QUALITY TIME ON HIGHWAY 1

Recent Doonesbury Books by G.B. Trudeau

Read My Lips, Make My Day, Eat Quiche and Die!
Give Those Nymphs Some Hooters!
You're Smokin' Now, Mr. Butts!
I'd Go With the Helmet, Ray
Welcome to Club Scud!
What Is It, Tink, Is Pan in Trouble?
Action Figure!

In Large Format

The Doonesbury Chronicles
Doonesbury's Greatest Hits
The People's Doonesbury
Doonesbury Dossier: The Reagan Years
Doonesbury Deluxe: Selected Glances Askance
Recycled Doonesbury: Second Thoughts on a Gilded Age

A DOONESBURY BOOK

by G. B. TRUDEAU

QUALITY TIME ON HIGHWAY 1

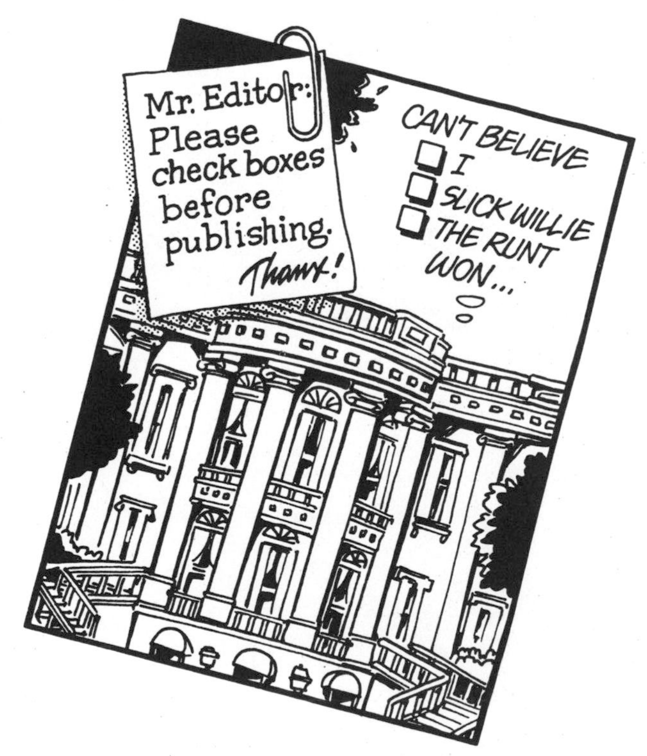

ANDREWS and McMEEL A UNIVERSAL PRESS SYNDICATE COMPANY KANSAS CITY

DOONESBURY is distributed internationally by Universal Press Syndicate.

ISBN: 0-8362-1712-8

Library of Congress Catalog Card Number: 92-75355

"It's weird out there, man."

— Former President George Bush

KENNEDY AIRPORT, PLEASE.
YOU GOT IT.

HOW LONG A DRIVE IS THAT?
FORTY MINUTES. MAYBE AN HOUR IF WE GET TRAFFIC.

BY THE WAY, I'VE GOT SOME PRETTY STRONG VIEWS ABOUT HOW THE MAYOR IS DOING. FOR A $5 FLAT FEE, I WON'T SHARE THEM WITH YOU ALL THE WAY OUT TO THE AIRPORT.

DEAL.
ENJOY THE RIDE.

REALLY? FOR FIVE BUCKS MORE, I GET PEACE AND QUIET ALL THE WAY TO THE AIRPORT?
YUP. I WON'T SAY WORD ONE ABOUT THE MAYOR!

NOR WILL I HOLD FORTH ON THE TYSON VERDICT, THE COPS OR THE WEATHER. I ALSO WON'T GET LOST, WON'T SPEED AND WON'T SCREAM AT MY DISPATCHER IN ARABIC.

WOW... WHAT A GREAT CONCEPT!
THANKS. CHECK OUT YOUR ARMREST ASHTRAY.

PEANUTS!
IT'S ALL PART OF MY AMBASSADOR CLASS SERVICE. ENJOY!

THIS ISN'T YOUR REGULAR LINE OF WORK, IS IT, MISS?
YOU GOT THAT RIGHT. I'M A PERFORMANCE ARTIST...

MY HUSBAND GOT THROWN OUT OF WORK, AND I WASN'T GETTING ANY GIGS, SO I'M DOING THIS UNTIL WE CAN GET THINGS GOING AGAIN.

WHAT'S YOUR HUSBAND IN?
ADVERTISING. HE'S DOING FREELANCE NOW. IN FACT, HE'S PRESENTING A BIG PRINT CAMPAIGN TO A NEW CLIENT TODAY.

NAH, IT'S GOTTA SAY **CLASS!** NITE-T-NITE ESCORT SERVICE **MEANS** CLASS!
HOW ABOUT IF I GIVE HER A TOP HAT?

THE CHICK DON'T LOOK CLASSY ENOUGH, KNOW WHAT I'M SAYING?
WE COULD GIVE HER A TOP HAT, SIR...

KIND OF A GINGER ROGERS THING — STYLISH, VIVACIOUS. BUT WITH A TOUCH OF NAUGHTI-NESS! I THINK THAT'S HOW YOU WANT TO POSITION YOURSELF.

THE PRINT ADS SHOULD MAKE PEOPLE THINK YOU'RE DIFFER-ENT, SPECIAL. YOU WANT THEM TO BELIEVE YOU REALLY **ARE** WHAT YOU SAY YOU ARE — A **LEGITIMATE** ESCORT SERVICE!

MAYBE WITH A PUSH-UP BRA...
WHATEVER. YOU AGREE WITH MY CONCEPT?
GB Trudeau

HEY, BABE! HOW'D THE MEETING WITH YOUR NEW CLIENT GO?
GREAT. I GOT THE ACCOUNT.

I ALSO LEARNED SOMETHING VERY VALUABLE TODAY, J.J. I LEARNED I DON'T **NEED** A MILLION-DOLLAR NATIONAL AC-COUNT TO VALIDATE WHAT I DO!

I LEARNED THERE'S **JUST** AS MUCH SATISFACTION AND DIGNITY IN A MODEST LOCAL CAMPAIGN! IT DOESN'T MATTER **WHAT** YOU SELL — IT'S HOW YOU SELL IT!
GB Trudeau

MY! WHAT EXACTLY ARE WE SELLING?
UM... CAREFULLY SCREENED HOSTESSES.

AN **ESCORT SERVICE?** YOU'RE DOING ADS FOR AN **ESCORT SERVICE?**
I'M MAKING THEM TASTEFUL, J.J.—BESIDES, WE NEED THE MONEY...

NOT **THAT** BAD, WE DON'T!
OH, GET **OFF** IT, J.J.! IN CASE YOU HADN'T NOTICED, THERE'S A **RECESSION** ON! YOU WANT ME TO JUST SIT AROUND?

MIKE, WHAT HAS **HAPPENED** TO YOU? DO YOU HAVE A **SHRED** OF PRINCI-PLES ANYMORE? YOU'RE NO BETTER THAN A... A...
A WHAT? **SAY** IT! A **WHAT?**
GB Trudeau

A **CAREFULLY SCREENED HOSTESS!**
THAT DOES IT! I'M OUT OF HERE!

WHY, MR. BELLOWS! WHAT A SURPRISE!
MIKE, I'LL COME RIGHT TO THE POINT. I'M RUNNING A CONSULTANCY NOW...

THE BUSH PEOPLE HAVE ASKED ME TO DEVELOP SOME NEW ATTACK ADS FOR THEM. GIVEN YOUR CAMPAIGN EXPERIENCE, I'D LIKE YOU ON BOARD FOR THIS, UNLESS YOUR PRIDE FORBIDS IT, OF COURSE.

MY PRIDE? HEE, HEE! DID YOU SAY MY **PRIDE?**

HA, HA, HA! HA, HA, HA! YUK!
GOOD. BE IN MY OFFICE IN AN HOUR.
©B Trudeau

YES?
HI, I'M MIKE DOONESBURY. I'VE GOT AN APPOINTMENT.

THAT'S NICE. WITH WHOM?
UM... MR. BELLOWS. YOUR BOSS.

I GOT A LOT OF BOSSES. I'M THE RECEPTIONIST FOR NINE DIFFERENT "CONSULTANTS" WHO TIME-SHARE ONE EXECUTIVE SUITE!
OH.
©B Trudeau

I HAVE TO KEEP UP THIS **COMPLETE** PRETENSE!
AND WHAT A FINE JOB YOU'RE DOING.

MR. BELLOWS?
DOONESBURY! COME ON IN! GOOD TO SEE YOU, SON!

NOT LIKE THE OLD DAYS, EH, KID? USED TO HAVE THREE FLOORS! NOW I HAVE ONE SUITE TWO DAYS A WEEK!
I'M SURE YOU'LL BOUNCE BACK, SIR.

WELL, LET'S HOPE WE BOTH DO. LET ME SEE WHAT YOU'VE BEEN WORKING ON LATELY.
WELL, SIR, I DON'T HAVE MUCH TO SHOW. JUST A LOCAL PRINT CAMPAIGN...

HMM... INTERESTING. IS THIS TRUE? ONLY $39.95 AN HOUR?
WELL, IT'S A LITTLE MISLEADING. YOU HAVE TO PAY FOR THE HOTEL ROOM.
©B Trudeau

WELL, KID, HERE'S THE DEAL. THE BUSH CAMPAIGN NEEDS ATTACK ADS—LOTS OF 'EM! FROM NOW ON, IT'S GOING TO BE DOWN AND DIRTY!

THINGS ARE TENSE. IN FACT THE WHITE HOUSE IS SO CONCERNED THEY'RE EVEN PUTTING SKIPPY BACK ON THE ROAD.
SKIPPY? WHO'S HE?

THE PRESIDENT'S EVIL TWIN. BUT IT'S ALL HUSH-HUSH. NOBODY'S SUPPOSED TO KNOW ABOUT HIM!

SO VOTE FOR ME! LET'S SEND THE NAZIS A MESSAGE!
HEY... IT'S SKIPPY!
HE'S BACK!

SO THE BASIC STRATEGY IS THAT BUSH'S EVIL TWIN, SKIPPY, WILL ATTACK FROM THE GROUND, AND WE'LL ATTACK FROM THE AIR!

IT COULD GET ROUGH, DOONESBURY. POLITICS HAS BECOME A CONTACT SPORT. DO YOU THINK YOU HAVE THE STOMACH FOR IT?

YES, SIR. I HAVE A FAMILY NOW. I'LL DO WHAT I HAVE TO.
WHAT IF I ASK YOU TO TAKE A REAL CHEAP SHOT AT BUCHANAN?

I'LL ASK "HOW LOW?" SIR.
YOU'VE CHANGED, KID. I LIKE THAT.

BASICALLY, WHAT THE WHITE HOUSE WANTS TO DO IS KEEP RETURNING TO THE GULF WAR. THAT'S WHERE BUCHANAN IS MOST VULNERABLE!

USING GENERAL KELLEY WAS OKAY, BUT WHAT WE REALLY NEED ARE SPOKESMEN THE PUBLIC CAN **IDENTIFY** WITH!

MY CONCEPT IS TO FIND TWO GULF WAR VETS—ORDINARY SOLDIERS FOR WHOM BUSH'S WAR WAS A DEFINING, EVEN TRANSFORMING, EXPERIENCE!

A BANK HEIST? I DUNNO, RAY...
JUST ONE, MAN! JUST TO TIDE US OVER!

IT WAS MIKE! HE WANTS TO USE ME IN A SPOT!
YOU'RE KIDDING! WHAT KIND OF SPOT?

A BUSH ATTACK AD! HE WANTS TO USE ORDINARY SOLDIERS FROM DESERT STORM TO POINT OUT HOW PAT BUCHANAN LET THEM DOWN...

I'M GOING TO BE ON NATIONAL T.V.!
INCREDIBLE! AND TO THINK I'M THE ACTOR OF THE FAMILY!

I BETTER GET MY HELMET WAXED!
I'LL IRON YOUR WAR TOGS!

HEY, RAY, YOU REMEMBER MY FRIEND MIKE DOONESBURY? THE GUY WE STAYED WITH IN NEW YORK? HE WANTS US TO MAKE SOME T.V. ADS!

HE NEEDS SOME GULF WAR VETS TO GO ON CAMERA AND TRASH PAT BUCHANAN FOR NOT SUPPORTING THE WAR EFFORT!

YOU GOT ANY PROBLEM WITH THAT? WE'D BE DOING THEM FOR THE BUSH CAMPAIGN.
FOR WHO?

BUSH? OUR FORMER COMMANDER-IN-CHIEF?
OH, SURE! THE OLD DUDE WHO'S ALWAYS POSING WITH SCHWARZKOPF?

THANKS FOR DOING THESE SPOTS, GUYS. I REALLY APPRECIATE IT.
ANYTHING FOR THE C-IN-C, MIKE!
WE'RE GETTING PAID, RIGHT, MAN?

ONLY SCALE, RAY. BUT THERE ARE OTHER REWARDS, LIKE GETTING TO TAKE OUT PAT BUCHANAN. LET'S GET BUSY, OKAY?

ACTUALLY, IT'S TOO BAD ABOUT BUCHANAN. IF HE HADN'T BEEN SUCH A WAR WEENIE, I MIGHT'VE VOTED FOR HIM.
CAN'T SAY I'VE BEEN FOLLOWING HIM. THINK I'D LIKE HIM?

NAH. HE'S A RACIST.
REALLY? IT'S COOL YOU CAN GET PAST THAT, MAN.

OKAY, RAY, LET'S DO IT! ROLL-IT!
HI. I'M RAY HIGHTOWER, DECORATED GULF WAR VETERAN.

YOU KNOW, WHEN I FIRST WENT TO WAR, I WAS PROUD TO BE SERVING MY COUNTRY! AND IT DIDN'T BOTHER ME THAT PEOPLE LIKE PAT BUCHANAN DIDN'T SUPPORT US.

THEN ONE DAY I TOOK A HIT. AS I LAY IN A POOL OF MY OWN BLOOD, ALL I COULD THINK WAS, "YO, THIS IS **FREEDOM'S** FIGHT! WHERE'S MR. CROSSFIRE WHEN THE GOING GETS **TOUGH**?"

IT STILL HURTS, MAN...
HEY! BUCHANAN! I WANT A **PIECE** OF YOU, MAN!

OKAY, B.D., YOU'RE UP. LET'S NOT USE THE SCRIPT. JUST GIVE ME YOUR FEELINGS.
OKAY...

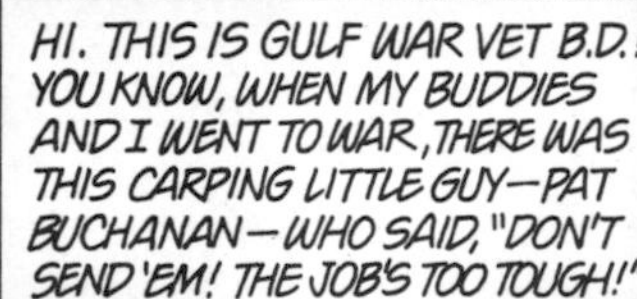
HI. THIS IS GULF WAR VET B.D.! YOU KNOW, WHEN MY BUDDIES AND I WENT TO WAR, THERE WAS THIS CARPING LITTLE GUY—PAT BUCHANAN—WHO SAID, "DON'T SEND 'EM! THE JOB'S TOO TOUGH!"

IT **WAS** TOUGH! BUT NOT ANY TOUGHER THAN COMING HOME TO A FULL-BLOWN RECESSION! WE **BLED** FOR OUR COUNTRY! AND NOW WE CAN'T EVEN GET **JOBS**! DOES BUSH CARE? **NOOO.** BUSH IS TOO DAMN BUSY TO...TO...UM...

OKAY, LET'S TAKE A FRESH LOOK AT THE SCRIPT.
WHAT HAPPENED?
YO, DON'T BLOW THIS, MAN. WE HAVEN'T BEEN PAID.

...AND THE SAME BUSH RESOLVE WE SAW IN DESERT STORM IS BOUND TO POP UP DOMESTICALLY! THE RECESSION? IT WON'T STAND! IT JUST WON'T! HE'LL FACE IT **DOWN**!

UNEMPLOYMENT? IT WON'T STAND! CRIME? IT WON'T STAND! DRUGS? NO WAY THEY'LL STAND! DECLINING EDUCATIONAL STANDARDS? THEY WON'T STAND!

PAT BUCHANAN'S CANDIDACY?
IT WILL NOT STAND! DOESN'T STAND A CHANCE!

CAN'T STAND THE HEAT!
I CAN'T STAND IT!
WE'VE LOST THEM. CUT!

JEREMY CAVENDISH! WHAT ARE YOU DOING OUT THERE?
GETTING MY NERVE UP, MRS. D! TO ASK YOU OUT AGAIN!
JEREMY, THAT'S THE SILLIEST THING I'VE EVER HEARD! YOU'RE GOING TO FREEZE TO DEATH!
I KNOW. PEOPLE STOP AND STARE, TOO, BUT THEY DON'T BOTHER ME. 'CAUSE THERE'S NOWHERE ELSE ON EARTH THAT I WOULD RATHER BE.
GOOD NIGHT, JEREMY.
WAIT! MRS. D! AT LEAST HEAR ME OUT! I PROPOSE AN EVENING OF PROFESSIONAL HOCKEY, COMPLETE WITH ALL THE WIENERS YOU CAN EAT! MY TREAT!
AND TO FURTHER SWEETEN THE POT, GUESS WHAT!
GO HOME, JEREMY.
I'M THINKING MARRIAGE! STEP-KIDS! THE WHOLE FIVE YARDS!
DON'T MAKE ME CALL THE POLICE, DEAR.
GBTrudeau

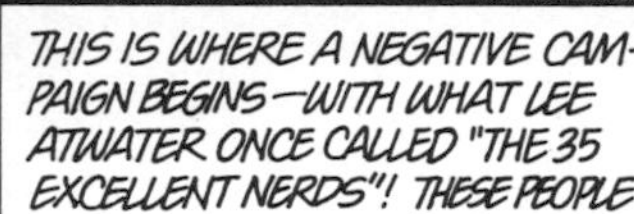

THIS IS ED ZIMMER, HEAD OF PERSONAL ANOMALIES, A NEW SECTION WE ADDED JUST THIS YEAR...

"PERSONAL ANOMALIES"?

THE WHITE HOUSE "OPO" UNIT. AN ELITE UNIT OF RESEARCH NERDS WHOSE MISSION IS TO FERRET OUT NEGATIVE INFORMATION ON BILL CLINTON...

ED ZIMMER IS OPO'S INFIDELITY SPECIALIST, RIGHT, ED?
THAT'S RIGHT, ROLAND. BASICALLY, MY JOB IS TO IDENTIFY BIMBONIC LIABILITIES.

BUT ISN'T BUSH A TAD VULNERABLE HIMSELF ON THAT ISSUE?
THAT'S NOT OUR CONCERN. WE DON'T DECIDE WHAT PLAYS. WE JUST LOCATE THE PLAYERS.

ANY LUCK?
NOT YET, BUT IT'S HOUSE-TO-HOUSE.

...AND THIS SECTION IS OUR MOST HEAVILY STAFFED. WE HAVE SIX SQUADS WORKING ON ACCESSING AND DUPLICATING EVERY PUBLIC RECORD FOR THE STATE OF ARKANSAS FOR THE LAST 13 YEARS!

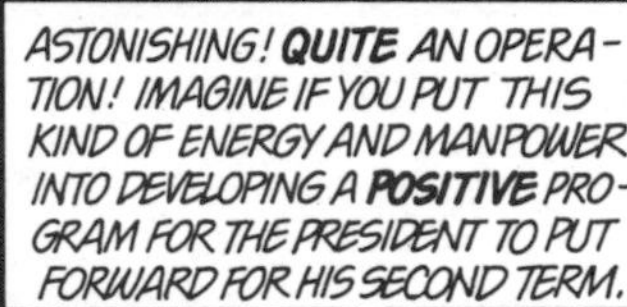
ASTONISHING! **QUITE** AN OPERATION! IMAGINE IF YOU PUT THIS KIND OF ENERGY AND MANPOWER INTO DEVELOPING A **POSITIVE** PROGRAM FOR THE PRESIDENT TO PUT FORWARD FOR HIS SECOND TERM.

UM... JUST A SUGGESTION. WE'LL EDIT IT OUT.
SURE YOU WILL.

MR. PRESIDENT? TAD WANAMAKER FROM OPO. YOU WANTED TO SEE ME?
YES, COME IN, TAD...

I'M GETTING SICK AND TIRED OF THIS CARPING LITTLE GUY COMING OUT OF ARKANSAS, HAD ENOUGH OF HIM. WHAT DO WE HAVE ON HIM? SUPPORT MY WAR?

AFRAID SO, SIR. HE MADE A STATEMENT BACKING THE GULF WAR AT THE VERY BEGINNING.

HMM... CAN IT BE TWISTED?
THE TECHNOLOGY EXISTS, YES, SIR.

I DON'T UNDERSTAND THIS...
WHAT'S THAT?

BY A WIDE MARGIN, VOTERS SAY THAT A CANDIDATE SHOULDN'T BE DISQUALIFIED BECAUSE HE'S HAD AN AFFAIR. BUT THEY ALSO SAY HE **SHOULD** BE DISQUALIFIED IF HE'S CAUGHT LYING.

IN OTHER WORDS, IT'S OKAY TO BE DUPLICITOUS — AS LONG AS YOU'RE HONEST ABOUT IT! WHAT KIND OF LOGIC IS **THAT?**

I MEAN, WHAT ON EARTH DO PEOPLE THINK AN AFFAIR **IS?** IT'S IMPLICITLY A **LIE!** YOU CAN'T HAVE IT BOTH WAYS.
YOU MEAN, IF I HAD AN AFFAIR, I'M AUTOMATICALLY A LIAR?

WELL, YES. WHY?
BECAUSE I HAD AN AFFAIR.

LIAR.
CAN'T WIN... MIGHT AS WELL HAVE ONE.

JERRY BROWN.
ONLY SMALL BILLS, PLEASE! I WANT TO BE ABLE TO IGNORE YOU LATER!
LOVE IT!

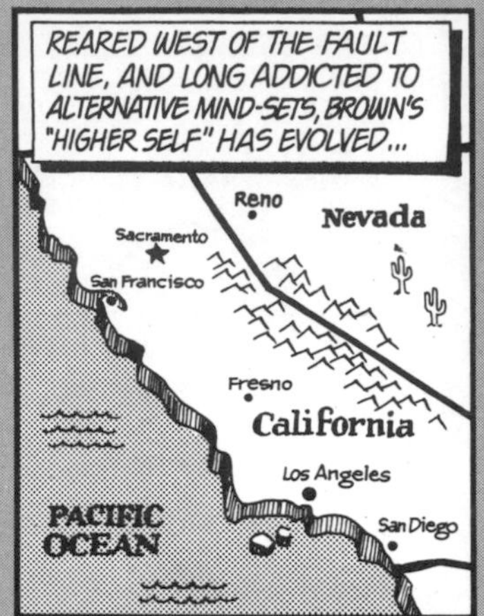
REARED WEST OF THE FAULT LINE, AND LONG ADDICTED TO ALTERNATIVE MIND-SETS, BROWN'S "HIGHER SELF" HAS EVOLVED...
Reno
Nevada
Sacramento
San Francisco
Fresno
California
Los Angeles
San Diego
PACIFIC OCEAN

...AND EVOLVED, TO THE POINT OF CONTINUOUS REINCARNATION. INDEED, IN A PREVIOUS LIFE, JERRY BROWN WAS ONCE...

JERRY BROWN.
ONLY LARGE BILLS, PLEASE! I WON'T FORGET YOU!
LOVE IT!
©B Trudeau

EXCUSE ME, FELLAHS, I'M DOING AN EXIT POLL FOR THE "POST." MIND TELLING ME WHO YOU VOTED FOR TODAY?
POLICE

JERRY BROWN.
ME, TOO!
ANY REASON IN PARTICULAR?

CLINTON'S TOO SLICK, TOO PAT!
YEAH, HE'S GOT ALL THESE GLIB ANSWERS!
AND BROWN'S NOT LIKE THAT?

NO WAY! JERRY'S GOT THE COURAGE TO MAKE NO SENSE AT ALL.
THAT'S RARE, MAN.
©B Trudeau

GOVERNOR BROWN, IN TAKING EXIT POLLS YESTERDAY, WE ASKED VOTERS WHAT THEY THOUGHT ABOUT YOU PERSONALLY...

CLEARLY MANY OF THEM IDENTIFIED WITH YOUR ANGER, BUT THAT VERY ANGER HAS MADE YOU SEEM COLD AND REMOTE TO THEM...

EVEN THOUGH THEY LIKE YOUR MESSAGE, VOTERS DON'T SEEM TO REALLY LIKE ... WELL... YOU.
©B Trudeau

AND I DON'T LIKE THEM! LOOK AT THE GOOFY CLOTHES I HAVE TO WEAR TO MEET THEM!
OH...SO YOU KNOW.

GOVERNOR BROWN, ISN'T THERE SOME DANGER IN CONSTANTLY ATTACKING GOVERNOR CLINTON ON THE CHARACTER ISSUE?

AFTER ALL, YOU HAVE SIMILAR CONTROVERSIES IN YOUR PAST, LIKE THE FAVORS YOU ALLEGEDLY DID FOR A MAJOR ORGANIZED-CRIME FIGURE WHO CONTRIBUTED TO YOUR CAMPAIGN...
©B Trudeau

DO YOU THINK IT WOULD BE FAIR IF SUCH EPISODES FROM **YOUR** RECORD AS GOVERNOR WERE RAISED DAILY BY THE CLINTON CAMPAIGN STAFF?

YOU GET HEALTH BENEFITS?
NO, NO, HE'S A VOLUNTEER!
OF WHICH YOU'RE A MEMBER, I TAKE IT.

MR. REDFERN? THIS IS TY SIMPKIN. I'M WITH THE BROWN CAMPAIGN. I'M NOT EXACTLY SURE WHAT MY TITLE IS HERE, BUT I'M PRETTY HIGH UP.
UH-HUH. WHAT CAN I DO FOR YOU, TY?

WELL, FIRST, I WANTED TO THANK YOU FOR YOUR PIECE TODAY!
UH... HAVE YOU READ IT? IT'S A PRETTY CRITICAL LOOK AT BROWN.

SURE, BUT THE IMPORTANT THING IS YOU TAKE HIM **SERIOUSLY** NOW! YOU'VE PLUGGED INTO JERRY'S CONSCIOUSNESS, ALLOWING **OTHERS** TO ACCESS HIS MESSAGE!
IF YOU SAY SO.

ANYWAY, WOULD YOU LIKE TO BE A STATE CO-ORDINATOR?
FOR WHICH JERRY?
©B Trudeau

THANKS FOR TURNING UP, EVERYBODY. IT LOOKS LIKE WE'VE GOT JUST ABOUT THE WHOLE UNIT HERE...

I DON'T HAVE TO TELL YOU THAT THE ARMY DRAWDOWN HAS CHANGED A LOT OF LIVES FOR THE WORSE. MANY OF US ARE UNEMPLOYED AND ARE GONNA STAY THAT WAY UNLESS WE TAKE CHARGE OF OUR LIVES!

WE'VE GOT TO COUNT ON EACH OTHER, JUST LIKE WE DID DURING DESERT STORM! WE'VE GOT TO NETWORK, OPEN DOORS FOR OUR BUDDIES, STARTING NOW! OKAY, WHO HERE HAS A JOB? SHOW OF HANDS...

SIGH...
I TOLD YOU.
GBTrudeau

OKAY, PLAN B. WE'RE THINKING OF STARTING A STREET GANG. ANY TAKERS?
I'M IN.
ME, TOO!

BOOPSIE! WHAT'S UP, BABE-O-RAMA?
GOOD NEWS, SID! B.D. AND I JUST DECIDED TO GET MARRIED! WE NEED YOUR HELP!

MY HELP? SWEETHEART, I DON'T DO PRE-NUPS...
NO, NO, WE NEED YOU TO **MARRY** US!

SAY WHAT?
DIDN'T YOU BUY ONE OF THOSE MAIL-ORDER MINISTRIES BACK IN THE '60s? TO GET OUT OF THE DRAFT?

DAMN, YOU'RE RIGHT! I'M SOME SORT OF HOLY MAN!
WELL, I THOUGHT SO! CAN WE BOOK YOU FOR TO-NIGHT?
©B Trudeau

HEY, KIDDO!
THANKS FOR COMING OVER, SID. SORRY ABOUT THE SHORT NOTICE.

NO PROBLEMO! BUT WHAT BROUGHT ALL THIS ON?
THE BABY. B.D. AND I WERE ARGUING OVER WHOSE LAST NAME HE WOULD HAVE...

AND THEN IT HIT US—WE SHOULD JUST GET MARRIED, AND LET HIM TAKE THE FATHER'S LAST NAME, LIKE OTHER KIDS!
SOUNDS REASON-ABLE...

WHAT **IS** YOUR LAST NAME?
D.
©B Trudeau

YOU CAN REALLY PERFORM A WEDDING CEREMONY, SID?
NO PROBLEMO! I'M A MAN OF THE CLOTH!

BACK IN THE '60s, YOU COULD GET A DRAFT DEFERMENT IF YOU WERE IN THE CLERGY. SO I SENT IN $3 TO THIS MAIL-ORDER MINISTRY...

FOUR DAYS LATER, I GOT BACK A CERTIFICATE SAYING I WAS A FULLY ORDAINED MINISTER IN THE CHRISTIAN ORDER OF IMMACULATE PACIFISM.

WHAT'D YOUR RABBI SAY?
DAD? BUMMED.
©B Trudeau

OKAY, GUYS, I'M READY.
HAPPY DAY— LET'S DO IT!

SHOULDN'T WE HAVE SOME SORT OF TEXT FOR THE CEREMONY?
NOT TO WORRY. I'VE GOT A BOOK OF COMMON PRAYER...

I LIFTED IT WHEN I WAS DOWN AT UNIVERSAL THIS MORNING.

YOU STOLE A PRAYER BOOK?
FROM A MOVIE STUDIO?
IT'S A PROP. I GOTTA HAVE IT BACK BY FIVE.

INCOMING FAX, J.J.! LOOKS LIKE ANOTHER BULLETIN FROM MALIBU...
WHRRRRRRRR!

WELL, WHAT DO YOU KNOW? A **WEDDING** ANNOUNCEMENT!
THE BABY MUST'VE TIPPED THE SCALES.

THINK THEY'LL GET THROUGH IT THIS TIME?
YEAH. IF THEY'RE NOT READY NOW, THEY'LL **NEVER** BE.

DEARLY BELOVED, WE... **WHOA!** MAJOR BEACH BABE AT TWO O'CLOCK!
WHERE?

OKAY, LET'S SEE... "WE ARE GATHERED HERE TOGETHER..." ETC., ETC.,... "IN HOLY MATRIMONY"... ETC., ETC. OKAY, LET'S CUT TO THE CHASE...

"IF ANYONE PRESENT KNOWS ANY REASON WHY THESE TWO SHOULD NOT BE MARRIED, LET THAT PERSON SPEAK NOW OR FOREVER HOLD HIS PEACE."

UM... I HAVE A REASON...
BOOPSIE!
WHAT'S THE PROBLEM, BOOPSIE?

I THINK MY WATER JUST BROKE.
OH, GROSS!
LOOK, KIDS, I'VE GOT A FIVE O'CLOCK.

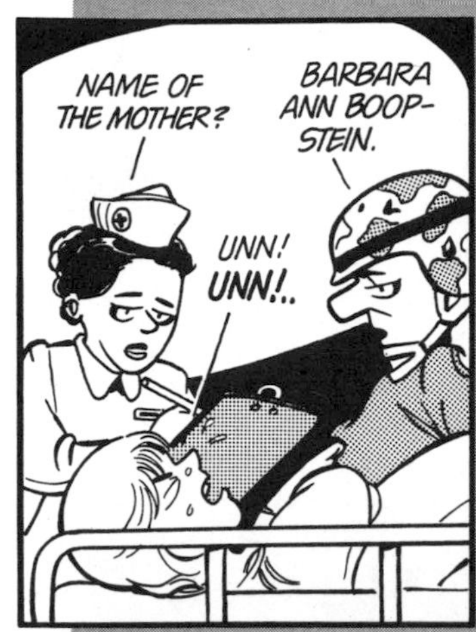
NAME OF THE MOTHER?
BARBARA ANN BOOPSTEIN.
UNN! **UNN!..**

AGE?
33.
BUT ON FILM, SHE PLAYS MID-TWENTIES.

MARRIED?
UM...
I NOW PRONOUNCE YOU HUSBAND AND WIFE!

YES.
YOU MAY KISS THE BRIDE, ALTHOUGH I WOULDN'T RECOMMEND IT.
AIEE!

WILL YOU BE ATTENDING THE BIRTH, MR. D?
UH...NO. I CAN'T REALLY HANDLE THAT STUFF.

LEAVE IT TO THE PROS— THAT'S WHAT I ALWAYS SAY!
ME, TOO. HOW LONG DO YOU THINK IT'LL TAKE, MA'AM?

HARD TO SAY. SHE'S PRETTY WELL DILATED. MAYBE FOUR HOURS...
FOUR HOURS? THAT LONG?

WANT TO HIT A MOVIE?
NAH. I BETTER STICK AROUND AND HELP WITH THE BILLS...

THIS IS GOING TO BE THE LONGEST FOUR HOURS OF MY LIFE...

I MEAN, WHILE WE'RE SITTING HERE, THIS BRAND-NEW LIFE, THIS INSANE MIRACLE, IS TAKING PLACE IN THE NEXT ROOM! IT'S JUST **INCREDIBLE!**

DID YOU BRING YOUR GAMEBOY?
IN THE CAR. YOU OUGHT TO GET SOME Z'S, THOUGH.

UNH! UNH!
THAT'S IT, BOOPSIE! BEAR DOWN! ALMOST THERE!...

GOOD LORD! THE BABY IS... IS...

WHAT? WHAT?
IT'S WEARING A HELMET!
YES! IT'S A BOY!
MR. D.? IT'S A GIRL!

HELLO, LADIES!
B.D.!

NICE JOB, KID!
YOU'RE NOT TOO DISAPPOINTED SHE'S NOT A BABY FULLBACK?

GET OUTA HERE — SHE'S PERFECT!
A PERFECT SAINT, IT TURNS OUT. HER HIGHER SELF JUST TOLD ME THAT IN HER PREVIOUS LIFE, SHE WAS MOTHER TERESA!

BOOPSIE, MOTHER TERESA'S STILL ALIVE.
WOW... SHE MUST BE LIKE A SCOUT OR SOMETHING.

BOOPSIE, I DON'T SEE HOW THE BABY COULD HAVE BEEN MOTHER TERESA IN ANOTHER LIFE. MOTHER TERESA'S STILL WITH US.
WELL, IT'S NOT IMPORTANT WHO SHE WAS, B.D., ONLY WHO SHE WILL BE!

SHE COULD BE A GREAT STAGE ACTRESS, OR A MAJOR FILM STAR, OR A FEATURED PLAYER OF A HIT, PRIME-TIME DRAMATIC SERIES...

...OR SHE COULD HAVE HER OWN TALK SHOW, OR BE A RECORDING ARTIST, OR SHE COULD HOST HER OWN SYNDICATED GAME SHOW!

OR FEED AND CLOTHE LEPERS.
I MEAN, ANYTHING'S POSSIBLE!

YOU GOT **MARRIED?** YOU'RE **KIDDING,** MAN!
I KNOW, I KNOW, IT DOESN'T SOUND LIKE ME, BUT I MET THIS TERRIFIC GIRL AT WORK...

SHE'S A MEDICAL CLAIMS ADJUSTOR — SMART, PRETTY, AND A WONDERFUL MOTHER TO OUR KIDS. I GOTTA SAY, I REALLY LUCKED OUT, MAN.

WOW...SOUNDS LIKE IT!
'COURSE, YOU HAVEN'T DONE SO BAD YOURSELF! I'VE BEEN FOLLOWING YOUR CAREER WITH GREAT PRIDE!

WELL, I GET A LOT OF HELP. DID YOU EVER MEET MIKE? THE MAN HIMSELF?
WHY, NO, I NEVER DID. WHAT'S HE LIKE, ANYWAY?

HEY, MIKE! COME OVER HERE!
HEY, NO, ZONK, I'M SURE HE'S GOT MORE IMPORTANT THINGS TO...
WHAT IS IT, Z?
GB Trudeau

MIKE, MEET THE GUY I'M MODELLED AFTER!
AN HONOR, MR. DOONESBURY!
NO KIDDING? I THOUGHT YOU WERE A COMPOSITE!

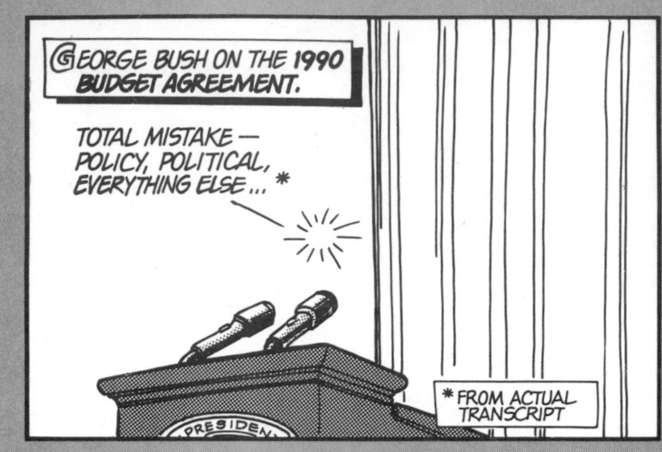
GEORGE BUSH ON THE 1990 BUDGET AGREEMENT.
TOTAL MISTAKE— POLICY, POLITICAL, EVERYTHING ELSE... *
*FROM ACTUAL TRANSCRIPT

POLICY BECAUSE IT SIMPLY DID NOT DO WHAT I THOUGHT—HOPED IT WOULD DO: CONTROL THIS—CONTROL— GET THIS ECONOMY MOVING...

THERE WERE SOME GOOD THINGS ABOUT IT, SO I CAN'T SAY—SHOULDN'T SAY— TOTAL MISTAKE.

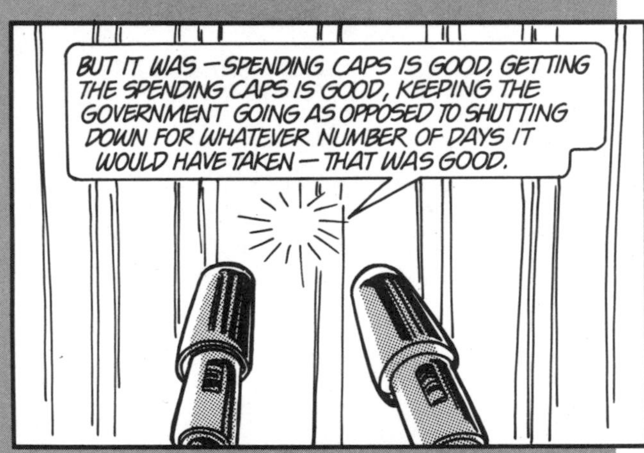
BUT IT WAS—SPENDING CAPS IS GOOD, GETTING THE SPENDING CAPS IS GOOD, KEEPING THE GOVERNMENT GOING AS OPPOSED TO SHUTTING DOWN FOR WHATEVER NUMBER OF DAYS IT WOULD HAVE TAKEN—THAT WAS GOOD.

BUT WHEN YOU HAVE TO WEIGH A DECISION IN RETROSPECT—HAVE THE BENEFIT OF HINDSIGHT— I WOULD HAVE TO SAY BOTH POLICY AND POLITICALLY, I THINK WE CAN ALL AGREE IT'S DRAWN A LOT OF FIRE.

IT WAS THE RIGHT THING TO DO, AND I TAKE FULL RESPONSIBILITY FOR IT.*
*MADE UP

DON'T WE HAVE A PARENTS' OPEN CLASS TODAY?
IT WAS YESTERDAY, DURING YOUR SHIFT. DON'T WORRY, ALEX IS DOING FINE.

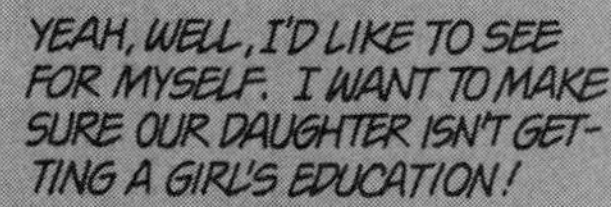
YEAH, WELL, I'D LIKE TO SEE FOR MYSELF. I WANT TO MAKE SURE OUR DAUGHTER ISN'T GETTING A GIRL'S EDUCATION!

A GIRL'S EDUCATION?

OKAY, WHO KNOWS THE ANSWER? JASON? ANDREW? JONATHAN? NICHOLAS?
MAYBE IF I WORE BRIGHTER COLORS...

OKAY, QUIET DOWN, EVERYONE! WHO KNOWS WHAT SEASON IT IS NOW? TEDDY?
SPRING!

VERY GOOD, TEDDY! WHAT MONTH IS IT? MICHAEL?
IT'S APRIL!

RIGHT! OKAY, WHO KNOWS WHAT DAY OF THE WEEK IT IS?
I DO! JULY!

NOPE. ANYONE ELSE? ROB, WE HAVEN'T HEARD FROM YOU! ALBERT? KEVIN?
WHAT'S THE DEAL HERE? MAYBE I NEED TO LOSE SOME WEIGHT.

HOW'S NURSERY SCHOOL GOING, HONEY?
OKAY, I GUESS. EXCEPT I NEVER GET TO SAY ANYTHING...

WHAT DO YOU MEAN, ALEX?
THE DORKY BOYS GET ALL THE ATTENTION. MRS. JASPER ISN'T FAIR ABOUT LETTING THE GIRLS ANSWER QUESTIONS.

HMM...

MAYBE I SHOULD HAVE A LITTLE TALK WITH HER.
MOM, SHE'LL NEVER CALL ON YOU! SEND DADDY.

MRS. DOONES-BURY! HOW NICE TO SEE YOU HERE!
I'M SORRY TO DISTURB YOU, MS. JASPER, BUT ALEX HAS COME TO ME WITH A PROBLEM.

MS. JAS-PER!
WHAT SORT OF PROBLEM, MRS. DOONES-BURY?
SHE FEELS THE BOYS GET MOST OF YOUR ATTEN-TION. SHE'S FEELING SHORT-CHANGED.

MS. JAS-PER!
JUST A MINUTE, ERNIE. MRS. DOONESBURY, THAT'S JUST CRAZY. AFTER ALL, I'M A FEMALE MYSELF. IF ANYTHING, I FAVOR THE **GIRLS**!

MS. JAS-PER!
WHAT **IS** IT, ERNIE?
YES, BY ALL MEANS, LET'S FIND OUT.

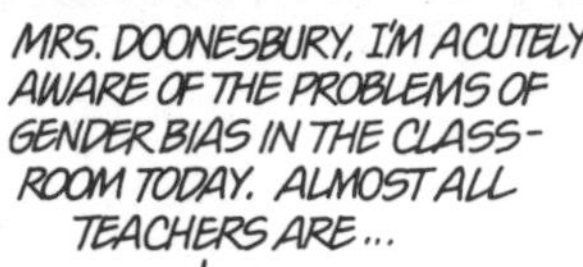
MRS. DOONESBURY, I'M ACUTELY AWARE OF THE PROBLEMS OF GENDER BIAS IN THE CLASS-ROOM TODAY. ALMOST ALL TEACHERS ARE...

BUT YOU WOULDN'T BELIEVE HOW FORCE-FULLY BOYS CAN PROJECT THEIR PRES-ENCE. THEY MAKE THEMSELVES VERY HARD FOR US TO IGNORE.
I UNDER-STAND, BUT IT CAN'T BE AT THE EX-PENSE OF THE GIRLS' SELF-ESTEEM.

THOSE EARLY, EMPOWERING INFLUENCES ARE SO IMPORTANT. IN MY CASE, I LEARNED FROM MY **MOTHER** TO BE TOUGH AND INDEPENDENT AND STAND ON MY OWN.

HOW'D SHE TEACH YOU?
WELL, BY...UM... ABANDONING ME. OKAY, BAD EXAMPLE.

I SPOKE TO ALEX'S TEACHER ABOUT GENDER BIAS TODAY...

A CHAT SHE WEL-COMED, NO DOUBT.
ACTUALLY, SHE WAS PRETTY COOL ABOUT IT, CONSIDERING.

I MEAN, BIAS IS A PRETTY HARD THING TO TALK ABOUT, MUCH LESS ADMIT TO.

DOES ANYONE THINK I IGNORE THE GIRLS? TEDDY?
SIGH...

SO, YOUNG MAN! WHAT'S YOUR MAJOR?
ECONOMICS, MA'AM...

I'M LOOKING FORWARD TO A CAREER IN BANKING! YOU CAN'T BELIEVE THE EDUCATION I'VE GOTTEN HERE! FIRST-RATE! JUST CRACKERJACK!

WELL, THAT'S NICE TO HEAR, DEAR. I'VE BEEN DREADFULLY WORRIED ABOUT HOW WELL OUR COLLEGES HAVE BEEN PERFORMING LATELY...
WELL, YOU DON'T HAVE TO WORRY ABOUT YOUR ALMA MATER, MA'AM, ESPECIALLY NOW THAT WE'VE GOTTEN OUR ACCREDITING SCARE BEHIND US!

WELL, THAT'S VERY REASSURING, DEAR HEART...
CAN I GET YOU ANYTHING ELSE, CONGRESSWOMAN?

NO, NO, I MUST BE GOING. WHAT DO I OWE YOU, DEAR HEART?
UM... YIKES... LEMME SEE, THAT'S TWO SHERRIES AT $2.75 EACH... THAT COMES TO... UH... $6.35!

SIGH...
HEY, THAT CHECK'LL CLEAR, WON'T IT, CONGRESSWOMAN? HA, HA! JUST KIDDING!
GB Trudeau

SPECIAL TREAT, BOYS AND GIRLS! TONIGHT WE'RE SHOOTING THE BULL WITH BILLIONAIRE POPULIST ROSS PEROT!

GOOD EVENING, MR. PEROT! HOW ARE YOU, SIR?
COULDN'T BE BETTER, SON!
GB Trudeau

MR. PEROT, I THINK YOU'LL AGREE THAT SO FAR YOU'VE HAD A FREE RIDE IN THE MEDIA. THAT, OF COURSE, WILL CHANGE BIG TIME IN THE MONTHS AHEAD.

WITH YOUR REPUTATION FOR BEING THIN-SKINNED, DO YOU...
CLICK!

OKAY, CAMPERS, ROSS PEROT HAS JUST CALLED BACK AND WE'RE NOW ON OUR BEST BEHAVIOR...

SIR, LET'S TALK POSITIONS...
LET'S NOT! PEOPLE DON'T WANT POSITIONS! THEY WANT ACTION! THEY WANT SOMEONE WHO CAN, PARDON MY FRENCH, KICK BUTT!

YES, SIR, BUT DOESN'T A SUCCESSFUL LEADER HAVE TO KNOW WHICH BUTTS TO KICK, HOW HARD, AND IN WHAT DIRECTION?

DETAILS! THE INDIVIDUAL BUTTS DON'T MATTER!
SO YOU WON'T BE TAKING NAMES?
GB Trudeau

YOU SEE, MY FRIEND, PEOPLE EXPECT ACTION FROM ROSS PEROT! THAT'S WHAT MY LIFE'S BEEN ALL ABOUT! LET ME GIVE YOU AN EXAMPLE...

IN 1978, TWO OF MY EMPLOYEES WERE JAILED IN IRAN. SO I HIRED A PARAMILITARY TEAM TO GO IN THERE, FOMENT A JAILHOUSE RIOT, AND GET OUR PEOPLE SAFELY OUT.

THE OPERATION WAS A BIG SUCCESS! AND YOU KNOW WHAT LESSON I DREW FROM THAT EXPERIENCE?

BUSINESSMEN SHOULD HAVE THEIR OWN ARMIES?
CORRECT. I'D OFFER TAX CREDITS TO CEO'S.
GB Trudeau

MR. PEROT, COULD YOU BE A LITTLE MORE SPECIFIC ABOUT HOW YOU WOULD PROPOSE TO WIN THE NATION'S DRUG WAR?

NO. SPECIFICS ARE FOR SMALL MINDS. AMERICA'S OWNERS WANT **BOLD** ACTION, NOT ANOTHER THUMB-SUCKING WHITE PAPER.

THE OWNERS OF THIS COUNTRY ARE GOING TO TAKE BACK THEIR STREETS, AND BELIEVE ME, IT **WON'T** BE PRETTY!
SOUNDS OMINOUS. ANY IMPLICATIONS FOR THE BILL OF RIGHTS?

THE WHAT?
THE OWNER'S MANUAL.
©B Trudeau

MR. PEROT, IF I COULD FOLLOW UP ON THE DRUG WAR ISSUE, IT'S BEEN REPORTED YOU ONCE SUGGESTED CORDONING OFF MINORITY NEIGHBORHOODS TO CONDUCT HOUSE-TO-HOUSE SEARCHES...
WELL, NOT EXACTLY...

WHAT I WAS TRYING TO SAY IS THAT IF YOU'RE FIXING TO MAKE A LAW ENFORCEMENT OMELETTE, YOU BETTER BE PREPARED TO BREAK EGGS, ESPECIALLY THE BAD ONES!

THE KIND OF CAMPAIGN I WOULD WAGE AGAINST DRUGS WOULD BE MASSIVE, RELENTLESS AND TOTAL! WE WOULD TAKE **NO** PRISONERS.

WELL, THAT SHOULD RELIEVE THE OVERCROWDING.
HEY, IT'S JUST A COLORFUL FIGURE OF SPEECH!
©B Trudeau

YOU'RE ON "ALL THINGS RECONSIDERED." GO AHEAD, CALLER!
YEAH, MAN, THIS IS MEL FROM BUFFALO. I WORK IN A 7-11 HERE...

I JUST HEARD PEROT TALKING ABOUT HOW HE HATES THE SYSTEM, BUT HE DOESN'T HAVE ANY ANSWERS OR POSITIONS, BUT THAT'S OKAY BECAUSE YOU CAN ALWAYS ORDER 'EM UP LIKE A STACK OF PANCAKES, OKAY?

WELL, AS I'M LISTENING TO THIS DUDE, SUDDENLY I FLASH ON SOMETHING...
WHAT'S THAT, MEL?
©B Trudeau

I'M QUALIFIED TO BE PRESIDENT, MAN!
EXCELLENT, MEL! WANT TO DECLARE RIGHT NOW?

MR. CALVERT? BILL AND GINA TUDDLE. WE'RE HERE ABOUT THE "F" YOU GAVE OUR SON IN HISTORY.
COME IN! COME IN, MR. AND MRS. TUDDLE!

WE DON'T UNDERSTAND THIS GRADE. WE'VE NEVER HAD ANY GRADE PROBLEMS WITH TED BEFORE!
HOW DO YOU MEAN? WHAT ABOUT ALL THE "C"S HE'S GOTTEN?

WHAT'S WRONG WITH "C"S? "C"S WERE GOOD ENOUGH FOR ME WHEN I WAS A KID!
IS THAT ALL YOU WANT FOR YOUR SON? "GOOD ENOUGH"? IS THAT WHY YOU'VE NEVER COME TO A PARENT-TEACHER CONFERENCE BEFORE?

BUT TED'S NEVER HAD AN "F" BEFORE.
HE DIDN'T GET AN "F" THIS TIME, EITHER. HE GOT ANOTHER "C." I WAS JUST TRYING TO SHAKE YOU OUT OF YOUR COMPLACENCY, TO GET YOU INVOLVED.

WHAT A SLEAZY TRICK!
YOU **HORRID** MAN! WE ALREADY TOOK THE TV OUT OF TED'S ROOM!
GBTrudeau

HEY, BOOPSIE, IT'S MIKE. HOW'RE YOU ALL MAKING OUT?

WELL, THE BABY'S DOING FINE, BUT WE MISS B.D...
WHY? WHERE'S B.D.?

YOU DIDN'T HEAR? HE GOT CALLED UP DURING THE RIOTS. HE AND RAY ARE STILL ON PATROL.
WHAT?

IS IT JUST ME, OR WAS KUWAIT LESS VIOLENT?
LEAST WE'RE WORKING AGAIN, MAN.

YOU WOULDN'T BELIEVE HOW THIS THING CAME DOWN FOR ME, MAN...

ONE MINUTE I'M STANDING OUT ON THE BACK PORCH, WATCHING THE FIRES, JUST SHAKING WITH RAGE OVER WHAT'S HAPPENING TO BLACK AMERICA...

THEN SUDDENLY THE PHONE RINGS, AND I'M CALLED UP...

SIX HOURS LATER, I'M GUARDING FREDERICK'S OF HOLLYWOOD.
HEY, IT'S A NATIONAL TREASURE, MAN.

YO, CHECK IT OUT. THEY'RE STILL SHOWING THE RODNEY KING TAPE...

MAN... NO MATTER HOW MANY TIMES I SEE THIS, IT STILL SICKENS ME.

WHAT WERE THOSE JURORS THINKING?
I DUNNO, MAN...

EXCUSE ME? YOU GUYS GUARDING THE T.V.?
YES!
CHILL, MAN, CHILL...

SO WHERE WE AT, MAN?
PICO. WE GOTTA HEAD SOUTH.

MAN...THE WHOLE STREET'S BOARDED UP!
YEAH, WELL, AT LEAST, THE AREA'S SECURE.

EXCEPT THAT BUILDING OVER THERE. THINK WE SHOULD CHECK IT OUT?
WHAT IS IT?

A SAVINGS AND LOAN.
TOO LATE. LOOTED YEARS AGO.

I'LL TELL YOU ONE THING, MAN, THIS COMMUNITY'S GOING TO HAVE TO GET MORE INTERESTED IN THE ELECTION...

BUSH HAS BEEN A DISASTER, AND PEROT WOULD BE EVEN WORSE. WE GOTTA GET BEHIND CLINTON BIG TIME!

CLINTON? ARE YOU SERIOUS?
WITH CLINTON, WE GOT A SHOT AT SOME KIND OF FUTURE. I BELIEVE THE MAN'S A HEALER.

BUT...BUT WHAT ABOUT GENNIFER WITH A "G"?
INCREDIBLY, SHE'S NOT A BIG ISSUE IN THE GHETTO.

YOU KNOW, RAY, EVERYTHING THAT'S GONE DOWN HERE HAS PUT **EVERYONE** ON THE DEFENSIVE...

IT'S, LIKE, EVEN WITH MY OWN BLACK FRIENDS, I FEEL LIKE I GOTTA CHECK TO MAKE SURE WE'RE STILL COOL.

YO, IF YOU GOTTA CHECK, MAYBE YOU'RE NOT.

I BETTER NOT, THEN.
COOL.

FOR MORE ON ROSS PEROT'S 60-DAY MEDIA OUTAGE, HERE'S ROLAND HEDLEY...
PETER, TONIGHT THE NATION'S AIR-WAVES SEEM AL-MOST BECALMED.

AS WE ENTER DAY 12 OF PEROT'S WITHDRAWAL FROM PUBLIC SCRUTINY, THE UN-CANDIDATE REMAINS IN ROUND-THE-CLOCK CONSULTATIONS WITH "LEADING AUTHORITIES"...

SOURCES CLOSE TO THOSE AU-THORITIES SAY THAT PEROT IS MAK-ING TREMENDOUS PROGRESS, AND EXPECTS TO KNOW WHAT HE STANDS FOR WITHIN THE WEEK. PETER?

ROLAND, WILL THERE BE SOME SORT OF STATEMENT?
YES, I BELIEVE A COLORFUL ONE-LINER IS BEING MADE AVAIL-ABLE.
©B Trudeau

CLIK!
CLIK!
CLIK!

HEY...
CLIK!
CLIK!

...THIS IS AMAZING!
©B Trudeau

PEROT'S NOT ON TELEVISION!
I KNOW. IT'S EERIE.

MAN! 60 DAYS OF CRAMMING WITH LEADING AUTHORI-TIES! I'LL BET THE OTHER GUYS HAVEN'T PUT IN THAT KIND OF TIME!
YOU KNOW WHAT I WOULD AD-VISE MR. PEROT TO DO, B.D.?

I'D TELL HIM TO FORGET ABOUT WASTING $100 MILLION ON MEDIA HE CAN GET FOR FREE, AND IN-STEAD MAKE 5,000 LOANS OF $20,000 EACH TO START OR REBUILD MINORITY-OWNED BUSINESSES IN L.A.!

YOU KNOW... THAT'S NOT A HALF-CRAZY IDEA, BOOPSIE.
I KNOW. THANK YOU.
©B Trudeau

HOW'D YOU THINK OF IT?
IN A PREVIOUS LIFE, I WAS A LEADING AUTHORITY.

GOOD EVENING, ROSS PEROT'S NEWS BLACKOUT CONTINUES TO MAKE NEWS TONIGHT. ROLAND HEDLEY HAS THE DETAILS.

PETER, IT'S DAY 15 OF PEROT'S MEDIA MORATORIUM, AND ALL SIGNS ARE THAT HIS PRESIDENTIAL CANDIDATE CRAM COURSE IS RIGHT ON SCHEDULE!

LEADING AUTHORITIES, WHO ARE DRILLING PEROT ON ECONOMICS, THE ENVIRONMENT, DEFENSE AND FOREIGN POLICY, SAY HE IS ONLY DAYS AWAY FROM DECIDING WHAT HE BELIEVES IN.

ROLAND, HAS PEROT PULLED ANY ALL-NIGHTERS?
NO, BUT HIS PEOPLE HAVE. HE KNOWS HOW TO DELEGATE.

PETER, ALTHOUGH PEROT IS WORKING FEVERISHLY TO PUT TOGETHER A PACKAGE OF POSITIONS, IT'S BY NO MEANS CERTAIN THAT HE NEEDS ONE...

PEROT IS GOOD AT TRANSFORMING LIABILITIES INTO ASSETS. JUST AS JERRY BROWN HAS REDEFINED HYPOCRISY AS "EVOLUTION" AND "PERSONAL GROWTH"...

...PEROT HAS STIGMATIZED POSITIONS AS SOMETHING THAT POLITICIANS HAVE! UP UNTIL NOW, HE'S BEEN ABLE TO MARKET HIS IGNORANCE AS POLITICAL PURITY.

SO STANDING FOR SOMETHING COULD QUEER HIS POPULARITY?
RIGHT. OF COURSE, PEROT'S A RISK-TAKER.

YES?
HI, I'M YOUR PAPER BOY, SIR. I'M HERE TO FIX THE DISHWASHER!

YES?
AVON CALLING! I'M HERE TO RENOVATE YOUR DEN.

YES?
FIRE DEPARTMENT, MA'AM. I'M HERE TO TUNE YOUR LAWNMOWER.

YES?
HI, I'M A SOFTWARE SALESMAN! I'M HERE TO FIX THE GOVERNMENT!

MR. PRESIDENT, AS YOU KNOW, GOVERNOR CLINTON HAS TAKEN A TERRIBLE BEATING THESE PAST FEW MONTHS OVER ALLEGATIONS OF MARITAL INFIDELITY...

SINCE THE ISSUE HAS BEEN INFLAMED IN PART BY YOUR SUPPORTERS, THE QUESTION HAS ARISEN AS TO WHETHER GOVERNOR CLINTON IS BEING HELD TO A STANDARD FROM WHICH YOU ARE EXEMPT...

WE IN THE PRESS ARE NATURALLY RELUCTANT TO PURSUE THIS DIFFICULT QUESTION UNTIL SUCH TIME AS YOU MAKE A STATEMENT, WHICH WOULD THEN, OF COURSE, BE SUBJECT TO ALL THE NORMAL RULES OF VERIFICATION.

IT IS THEREFORE MY PAINFUL DUTY, AS DETERMINED BY LOT, TO ASK YOU THE FOLLOWING DIRECT QUESTION: MR. PRESIDENT, HAVE YOU EVER HAD AN EXTRAMARITAL AFFAIR?

NO.
GBTrudeau

LET'S GO!
CATCH YOU LATER, SIR.

"...AND HE WOULD SAY THINGS ABOUT INDIVIDUAL PEOPLE'S ANATOMY. I REMEMBER SPECIFICALLY HIM SAYING THAT ONE WOMAN HAD A BIG A--."

REMEMBER, DEAR HEARTS, WE ARE HEARING EXCERPTS FROM AN INTERVIEW* WITH ANGELA WRIGHT ABOUT HER FORMER BOSS, CLARENCE THOMAS...
*CONDUCTED BY SENATE AIDES OCT. 10, 1991.

MS. WRIGHT IS RECALLING AN INCIDENT INVOLVING JUSTICE THOMAS...
"I SPECIFICALLY RECALL BEING AT A SEMINAR..."

"... WHEN CLARENCE THOMAS COMMENTED ON THE DRESS I WAS WEARING AND ASKED ME WHAT SIZE MY B---- WERE."

EXCUSE ME, DEAR, WE CAN'T PERMIT ALL THESE HYPHENS.
THE HYPHENS SHALL BE STRICKEN FROM THE RECORD!

"IN GENERAL, GIVEN THE OPPORTUNITY, CLARENCE THOMAS WOULD SAY TO ME..."
THE ANGELA WRIGHT TESTIMONY* YOU NEVER HEARD. OF COURSE, THAT DIDN'T PREVENT SENATOR SIMPSON FROM ATTACKING MS. WRIGHT ANYWAY.
* GIVEN TO SENATE AIDES OCT. 10, 1991.

"'YOU NEED TO BE DATING ME, I THINK I'M GOING TO DATE YOU, YOU'RE ONE OF THE FINEST WOMEN I HAVE ON MY STAFF... WE'RE GOING TO BE GOING OUT EVENTUALLY...'"

"I SAW ANITA HILL ON TELEVISION MONDAY NIGHT, AND MY CONSCIENCE STARTED BOTHERING ME, BECAUSE I KNEW I FELT FROM MY EXPERIENCE WITH CLARENCE THOMAS THAT HE WAS QUITE CAPABLE OF DOING WHAT SHE SAID."

"I TH AS U LEGA DEFINI SEXUA HARASSMENT...
I MEAN, WASN'T ANYONE LISTENING TO THIS DEAR GIRL? IT'S A PERFECT OUTRAGE TO ALL WOMEN THAT NOT A
UH... LACEY?

"SHE CONFIDED TO ME INCREASINGLY THAT SHE WAS A LITTLE UNEASY, AND SHE GREW MORE UNEASY WITH THE CHAIRMAN..."
IS ANGELA WRIGHT CREDIBLE? LISTEN TO CO-WORKER ROSE JORDAIN'S CORROBORATION.*
*GIVEN TO SENATE AIDES ON OCT. 13, 1991.

"...BECAUSE OF COMMENTS SHE TOLD ME THAT HE WAS MAKING CONCERNING HER FIGURE, HER BODY, HER B------..."
MS. JORDAIN'S TESTIMONY, INEXPLICABLY, WAS NEVER ENTERED INTO THE RECORD, AS HAD BEEN PROMISED.

"SHE TOLD ME HE HAD COME TO HER HOME ONE NIGHT UNANNOUNCED... ONE TIME SHE CAME TO MY OFFICE IN TEARS..."
MORE TESTIMONY THAT THE WHITE HOUSE SIMPLY DIDN'T WANT YOU TO HEAR!

IT'S APPEARING WHERE?
IN THE COMICS, SIR. IT'S A LOW-TECH LYNCHING.

MORNING, 'RENTS! YOU'RE PROBABLY WONDERING ABOUT MY ROOM. RIGHT?
SUGAR POPS

YOUR ROOM?
YOU DIDN'T NOTICE? I'VE MOVED OUT OF IT!

YOU WHAT?
MOVED OUT! PACKED UP ALL MY STUFF...

YOU CAN'T RELIVE YOUR CHILDHOOD FOREVER, DAD. SOONER OR LATER, YOU'VE GOT TO GROW UP AND MOVE OUT!
THWIP! THWIP!
PLOP!
PLOP!

YOU DO?
REALLY?
SURE.

IT'S... IT'S A MIRACLE!
I TOLD YOU IF WE SWITCHED RELIGIONS...
ANYWAY, I'LL BE HAPPIER IN THE TV ROOM. DAD, CAN I SEND AWAY FOR THIS DECODER RING?
SUGAR POPS
©GB Trudeau

A ROUTINE SCREENING OF THE FEATURE FOR FAMILY VALUES.
HI, FOLKS. TELL US ABOUT YOURSELVES.

UM... OKAY. WE'RE THE REDFERNS. RICK AND I HAVE BEEN HAPPILY MARRIED FOR WHAT, TWELVE YEARS, HONEY?
YUP! PLUS THE FIVE YEARS WE LIVED TOGETHER!

WHAT?
WELL, SEE, I HAD TO BE SURE. I'D BEEN DIVORCED...
ALSO, SHE WAS TRYING TO GET HER CAREER GOING...

THAT'S IT! TAKE A HIKE! OUT!
YOU HAD TO MENTION THE CAREER.
TROT OUT THE KID, YOU SAID, WE CAN'T MISS!
SURE, BLAME ME.

ROUTINE FAMILY VALUES CHECK, FOLKS. WON'T TAKE A MINUTE.
NO PROBLEM. FIRE AWAY!
STOP SUCKING UP, MIKE.

GOT A FAMILY?
SURE DO! A BEAUTIFUL LITTLE GIRL! LOOK...
WHICH DOESN'T MEAN WE'RE NOT FOR A WOMAN'S RIGHT TO CHOOSE.

TOO BAD. YOU'RE OUT OF HERE.
WHAT? JUST BECAUSE WE'RE PRO-CHOICE?
WHAT IS THIS, CULTURAL PURIFICATION WEEK?

ADIOS.
AFTER 22 YEARS?
HEY, YO, WHOSE NAME IS UP THERE? HE'S THE FRANCHISE!

NICE-LOOKING COUPLE. LET'S CHECK OUT THEIR VALUES.
YOU FOLKS MARRIED?

YOU BET. WE TIED THE KNOT JUST THIS YEAR.
AND NOW WE'RE LOOKING FORWARD TO RAISING A FAMILY!

GREAT. WHERE?
RIGHT HERE IN MALIBU.
I'M IN SHOW BUSINESS. I WANT TO WORK CLOSE TO HOME!

HOLLYWOOD ELITE. NEXT!
NO... NO, IT'S NOT LIKE THAT! WE'RE FROM THE CHARLTON HESTON WING!
HE'S GOT A GUN! GO GET YOUR GUN, HONEY!

WE REGRET TO INFORM OUR READERSHIP THAT...

...NOT A SINGLE CHARACTER HAS PASSED OUR FAMILY VALUES EVALUATION EXAM.

ACCORDINGLY, THIS FEATURE WILL BE TEMPORARILY SUSPENDED...

THIS FEATURE

CONDEMNED

BY ORDER OF

THE COMMISSIONER OF COMICS

HI, HONEY!
HI, DREAM-BOAT! WHAT'S HAPPENING?

MY MARRIAGE, FOR ONE THING!
HEE, HEE! WHAT DO YOU WANT TO DO TODAY?

I DUNNO— WHAT DO **YOU** WANT TO DO?
I'VE GOT AN IDEA! LET'S GO DOWNTOWN AND HURL EPITHETS AT PEOPLE DIF-FERENT FROM US!

WE HAVE A **NEW** WRITER, I TAKE IT.
HEY, AT LEAST WE'RE BACK.
Diego Tutweiller

WHAT'S IN THE PAPER, HONEY?
THE USUAL— SINGLE MOTHERS WHO WORK, HOMOSEXUALS WHO TEACH, PEOPLE WHO GET AIDS...

YOU KNOW, MAYBE IT'S TIME WE MOVED TO THE SUBURBS!
GOOD IDEA! MORE OF US...

...AND LESS OF **THEM!**
A PLACE WHERE WE CAN PRAC-TICE OUR VALUES IN PEACE AND QUIET!

WHO **IS** THIS GUY?
I DON'T KNOW. I JUST WISH HE'D GET MY NOSE RIGHT!
Diego Tutweiller

DADDY! DADDY! **GREAT** NEWS!

WHAT IS IT, SQUIRT?
THEY'RE GIVING THE OLD WRITER ANOTHER CHANCE...

THERE'S GOING TO BE ONE FINAL FAMILY VALUES TEST! I FORGET WHAT IT'S CALLED, BUT THEY HAVE TO DIP THE FEATURE IN WATER OR SOMETHING...

A LITMUS TEST?
THAT'S IT! IF WE DON'T TURN PINK, WE'RE HOME **FREE!**
Diego Tutweiller

BEAR WITH US.

JUST TRYING OUT...

A FEW PRELIMINARY TEST SKETCHES...

...FOR THE CLINTON WHITE HOUSE.

WHAT CLINTON WHITE HOUSE?

TOUCHY.
GB Trudeau

B.D.?
HEY, BABE. WHAT'S UP?

I WAS JUST CALLING TO SEE HOW WORK WAS GOING...
GREAT. I LOVE THIS JOB...

I LOVE THE HOURS, I LOVE BEING OUT-DOORS, AND I LOVE GETTING IN PEO-PLE'S FACES...

SPEAKING OF WHICH, DO YOU HAVE ANY IDEA HOW FAST YOU'RE GOING?

HEY, WILL YOU PLEASE **STOP** THAT, B.D.? IT GIVES ME THE CREEPS!
©B Trudeau

SORRY, BABE. PULL OVER.
I'M **WARNING** YOU, B.D. ...
CHP
CALIFORN

GOOD MORNING, OFFICER! WHAT'S THE PROBLEM?
MAY I SEE YOUR DRIVER'S LICENSE, PLEASE, SIR?

UM.., SURE. WHY NOT?
DO YOU HAVE ANY IDEA HOW FAST YOU WERE GOING, SIR?

LOOK, OFFICER, CAN'T WE MAKE THIS GO AWAY?
THAT VOICE SOUNDS VERY FAMILIAR...
WOULD YOU STEP OUT OF THE VEHICLE, PLEASE, SIR?

B.D.?
OUT! AND SPREAD 'EM!

B.D.? IT'S ME, SID!
WOULD YOU STEP OUT OF THE VEHICLE, PLEASE, SIR?

HOW LONG YOU BEEN A CHIP, BABE?
SIR, I'M ASKING YOU TO STEP OUT OF YOUR VEHICLE.

HEY, C'MON, B.D., GIMME A BREAK HERE! I'M GOING TO LOSE MY LICENSE!
HEY, RAY! BRING ME THE STUN GUN!

THIS WOULDN'T BE HAPPENING IF I WERE A BABE, RIGHT?
THIS IS CALIFORNIA, SIR. BABES ARE PROTECTED BY STATE CHARTER.

HEY, C'MON, B.D., I'LL LOSE MY LICENSE! YOU CAN'T GIVE ME A TICKET!
SORRY, SIR.

YOU SCUMBAG! YOU'LL BE SORRY! YOUR DINGBAT WIFE IS NOW DEAD IN THIS TOWN! DEAD!
HEY, YOU TRASH BOOPSIE'S CAREER, AND UNIFORM OR NO, I'LL HUNT YOU DOWN LIKE A DOG!

HELLO...
WHAT?

GREAT MOVIE PREMISE! COP STOPS HIS BUDDY FOR SPEEDING...
HAVE A NICE DAY, SIR.

GUESS WHO I NAILED TODAY ON THE VENTURA FREEWAY — SID!

SID? YOU GAVE SID A TICKET?
HAD TO. FOOL BLEW BY ME AT 105 M.P.H.!

BUT HE'LL LOSE HIS LICENSE! HE WON'T BE ABLE TO DRIVE TO WORK! HE'LL HAVE TO TAKE THE BUS!
SO?
GB Trudeau

DON'T YOU SEE? YOU STRIPPED HIM OF HIS **MANHOOD!**
OF COURSE I DID! THAT'S MY JOB!
FZT!

B.D., **HOW** COULD YOU TICKET POOR SID? YOU'VE KNOWN HIM FOR YEARS!
I CAN'T PLAY FAVORITES, BABE.

OH, YEAH? HOW MANY OTHER PEOPLE DID YOU NAIL TODAY?
LOTS...

I HAD TWO HIGH-SPEED CHASES, ONE GUY WITH A BROKEN TAIL LIGHT, ONE RECKLESS DRIVING, AND TWO UNDER-THE-INFLUENCES.

I ALSO LET 23 BABES OFF WITH FRIENDLY WARNINGS.
WHAT, YOU HAVE A QUOTA?
GB Trudeau

LET ME GET THIS STRAIGHT. YOU LET OFF **ALL** BABES?
OF COURSE NOT. BABES WITH ATTITUDE GET CITATIONS.

BUT THE REST GET A PASS?
AS A COURTESY! BABES ARE IMPORTANT TO THE STATE ECONOMY. BESIDES, IT'S A LONG CHIP TRADITION. LOOK AT THIS PHOTO IN THE RECRUITMENT BROCHURE...

BUT SHE'S GETTING A TICKET!
NO, NO, SHE'S GIVING HIM HER PHONE NUMBER.
GB Trudeau

I'VE BEEN THINKING A LOT ABOUT POPPY'S BIG TOP LATELY...

THE G.O.P. SURE HAS BEEN THROWING A LOT OF FOLKS OUT OF THEIR TENT THIS YEAR...

IF YOU'RE GAY, THEY DON'T WANT YOU. IF YOU'RE PRO-CHOICE, FORGET IT. IF YOU CHERISH THE ENVIRONMENT, TAKE A HIKE...

IF YOU'RE A WORKING WOMAN, YOU'RE NOT THEIR KIND OF GAL. IF YOU'RE NON-WHITE, DROP DEAD!

IT SORT OF MAKES YOU CURIOUS, DOESN'T IT? I MEAN, WHO'S **LEFT**?
©B Trudeau

WHAT'S WRONG, SIR?
NOTHING, DANNY. GO TO SLEEP.

RAY! I DIDN'T KNOW YOU WERE HERE!

I JUST CAME OVER FOR THE GAME. I GOTTA LEAVE SOON...!
ARE YOU SURE? CAN'T YOU STAY FOR DINNER?

HEE, HEE! NO, THANKS. THIS MUST BE SORT OF A FANTASY COME TRUE FOR YOU, EH, BOOPSIE?
HOW'S THAT, RAY?
©B. Trudeau

TWO OFF-DUTY COPS IN YOUR LIVING ROOM?
UM... WELL, I DO FEEL SAFE.
>BURP!<

SO, RAY, HAVE YOU BEEN AS CONSCIENTIOUS ABOUT PULLING OVER SPEEDING BABES AS B.D.?
BABES?

OH, SURE. GOT TO. MOST OF 'EM ARE BWA's, AND THEY GOTTA BE TICKETED!
WHAT'S A BWA?

BABE WITH ATTITUDE.
BUT LAST WEEK, I STOPPED AN ABSOLUTELY MAGNIFICENT BWP!
©B. Trudeau

BABE WITH...?
POTENTIAL!
I DON'T STOP BWP's MYSELF. BEING MARRIED AND ALL.

WELL, I BETTER GET ROLLIN'! BIG DATE TONIGHT!

YOU'RE SEEING SOMEONE, RAY?
ABSOLUTELY I'M SEEING SOMEONE! AND SHE'S FINE!

SHE'S HOT FOR ME, TOO! SHE SAYS SHE WANTED ME FROM THE START! FROM MY OPENING LINE!
WHICH WAS?

"PULL OVER."
I'M REPORTING YOU GUYS.
©B. Trudeau

SO RAY'S FINALLY GOT A GIRLFRIEND?
YUP. HER NAME'S MAY...

SHE'S COOL—PRETTY, GOOD JOB, AND DIVORCED LIKE RAY. ONLY ONE DOWN SIDE...

AND THAT WOULD BE?
THAT WOULD BE A KID.

WHAT'S UP, LITTLE BRO?
YO, **MAMA**! THE PIG'S HERE!

YOUR MAMA READY, DESMOND?
WHO KNOWS, MR. CHIP? YO, CHECK THIS OUT—IT'S FROM MY MAN TUPAC!

"COP ON MY TAIL SO I BAIL 'TIL I DODGE THEM... THEY FINALLY PULL ME OVER AND I LAUGH... REMEMBER RODNEY KING, AND I BLAST **HIS PUNK**---!"

"WHAT THE ---- WOULD **YOU** DO? DROP THEM OR LET THEM DROP YOU! I CHOOSE **DROPPIN' THE COP!**"

SO! YOU'RE INTERESTED IN MUSIC.
MAMA SAID TO ENTERTAIN YOU. WANNA HEAR IT AGAIN?

UM...DES? COULD YOU TELL YOUR MAMA I'M HERE?
WHY DONCHA BREAK DOWN HER DOOR AND TELL HER YOURSELF, COP?

HERE I AM, BABY. SORRY I TOOK SO LONG.
HEY, WORTH THE WAIT, SUNSHINE!

COME HERE, YOU!
SMOOCH!
YOU GOT IT!
YO, IF YOU BE GETTIN' BUCK WILD, I'M ROLLIN'!

DON'T MIND MY LITTLE LIFESTYLE CHOICE.
HE WAS A **CHOICE**?
YOUR MAMA, MAN! YOURS TOO, MAMA!

ARNIE? BOOPSIE! I WONDER IF YOU'VE HAD A CHANCE TO LOOK OVER THE SCRIPT I SENT YOU LAST WEEK...

NO, NOT YET. BUT FRANKLY, BABE, I DON'T THINK IT'S RIGHT FOR US...
RIGHT FOR YOU? ARNIE, THIS IS A VERY SPECIAL PROJECT, A PRESTIGE PROJECT...

A PRESTIGE PROJECT? "THE MARLA MAPLES STORY"? HA, HA, HA! C'MON, BABE, GIMME A BREAK!
YOU LAUGH?

UH-OH...
YOU DARE LAUGH? FOOL! YOU ARE AS CARRION! IF YOU IGNORE MY ENTREATIES, RAVENS WILL PLUCK MAGGOTS FROM YOUR BRAINPAN AS YOUR LIFELESS FORM TWISTS FROM A PALM TREE IN BURBANK!

UH...OKAY, OKAY, CALM DOWN. I'LL TAKE A LOOK AT IT, OKAY?
COOL! THANKS A MIL, ARNIE!

YOU ASKED HUNK-RA TO CO-PRODUCE, DIDN'T YOU?
B.D., I HAD TO. I NEED HIS NEGOTIATING SKILLS.
GBTrudeau

GUESS WHO'S BACK, CAMPERS! WORLD-CLASS FRINGE CANDIDATE **ROSS PEROT!** CAN YOU HEAR ME, MR. PEROT?
CLEAR AS A BELL, SON.

SIR, LAST MONTH YOU TOLD THE SENATE YOU HAD FRESH EVIDENCE OF VIETNAM P.O.W.S...
THAT'S RIGHT. 59 OF 'EM!

UM... YOU SAID 30 AT THE TIME, SIR.
LET'S NOT PLAY GOTCHA! I SAID AT **LEAST** 30! I COULD BRING HOME 30 WITHOUT BREAKING A **SWEAT!**

OKAY, 59. WHEN ARE THEY COMING HOME?
AS SOON AS I CAN RUN CREDIT CHECKS ON THEM. STRICTLY ROUTINE. NO BIG DEAL.

MR. PEROT, AS YOU NOW KNOW, RUNNING FOR PRESIDENT CAN BE PRETTY ROUGH...

I'M WONDERING HOW YOUR FAMILY FEELS ABOUT YOUR JUMPING BACK INTO THE FRAY.
THEY LOVE IT! THEY'RE ALL ON BOARD! ESPECIALLY MY WIFE.

ARE YOU SURE, SIR? THE DAY YOU DECLARED, I THOUGHT HER FACE SAID IT ALL.
WHAT DO YOU MEAN? WHAT'D IT SAY?

IT SAID, "I'M MARRIED TO A PSYCHOTIC, AND THERE'S NOT A DAMN THING I CAN DO ABOUT IT."
SHE'S A SAINT. A WORLD-CLASS SAINT.

MR. PEROT, A LOT OF YOUR SUPPORTERS ARE DISTRESSED BY THE GROWING EVIDENCE OF YOUR BIGOTRY...

MY **BIGOTRY?** THAT'S CRAZY! MINNIE MOUSE COLESLAW! BONKERS! PRESS MYTH NO. 1,173!

THEN WHY DID YOU TRY TO KEEP YOUR DAUGHTER FROM MARRYING A JEW, REPORTEDLY SAYING, "YOU NEED TO HAVE YOUR CHILDREN LOOK LIKE YOU"? I MEAN, I FIND THAT INCREDIBLE!

WHY? BECAUSE OF MY EARS? **THAT'S** LOW! ARE YOU A JEW?
MUST BE. I'M IN THE MEDIA.

MR. PEROT, IT'S BEEN REPORTED RECENTLY THAT YOU TRIED TO DISCREDIT YOUR DAUGHTER'S JEWISH FIANCE BECAUSE, AS YOU PUT IT, "YOU DON'T THINK THAT I'D LET MY DAUGHTER MARRY A JEW."

SIR, DO YOU THINK...
THAT'S A FAIRY TALE! DAISY DUCK SALAD! NEVER HAPPENED! YOU KNOW, THIS ISN'T FUN ANYMORE! I'VE HAD IT! I'M DROPPING OUT!

YOU'RE... DROPPING OUT?
I'M GONE! OUT THE DOOR! END OF STORY! ADIOS!

UM... OKAY. OUR GUEST TONIGHT HAS BEEN...
I'M BACK! SIMPLE AS THAT! LET'S TALK ABOUT THE ISSUES!
©B Trudeau

MR. PEROT, I WONDER IF WE COULD TALK ABOUT THE VIETNAM WAR MEMORIAL FOR A MOMENT...

IT'S BEEN REPORTED THAT YOU SO DETESTED THE FINAL DESIGN THAT YOU HAD THE ORGANIZERS INVESTIGATED AND HARASSED...

HERE'S THE DEAL: IT'S A COMPLETE FAIRY TALE! NEVER HAPPENED!
AND THAT YOU OFTEN REFERRED TO THE MONUMENT'S ASIAN-AMERICAN DESIGNER AS "EGGROLL"!
©B Trudeau

BONKERS! CRACKERS! MICKEY MOUSE SUSHI!
TEST, TEST! TELL MR. P THE TAP'S ON!

MR. PEROT, DO YOU THINK IT'S PROPER, INDEED LEGAL, TO INVESTIGATE THE CREDIT RATINGS OF YOUR VOLUNTEERS?

NO. 1, OKAY? NOW, LET ME FINISH. NO. 1, THEY WERE ROUTINE INVESTIGATIONS. END OF STORY. NEXT QUESTION.
BUT...

LOOK, PEOPLE WERE CALLING DALLAS TO SAY, "WE'VE GOT CRIMES GOING ON DOWN HERE, THEFT, PEOPLE ARE STEALING FROM US!" WHAT WAS I SUPPOSED TO DO?
©B Trudeau

CALL THE POLICE?
NO. 1, OKAY? LET ME FINISH. NEXT QUESTION.

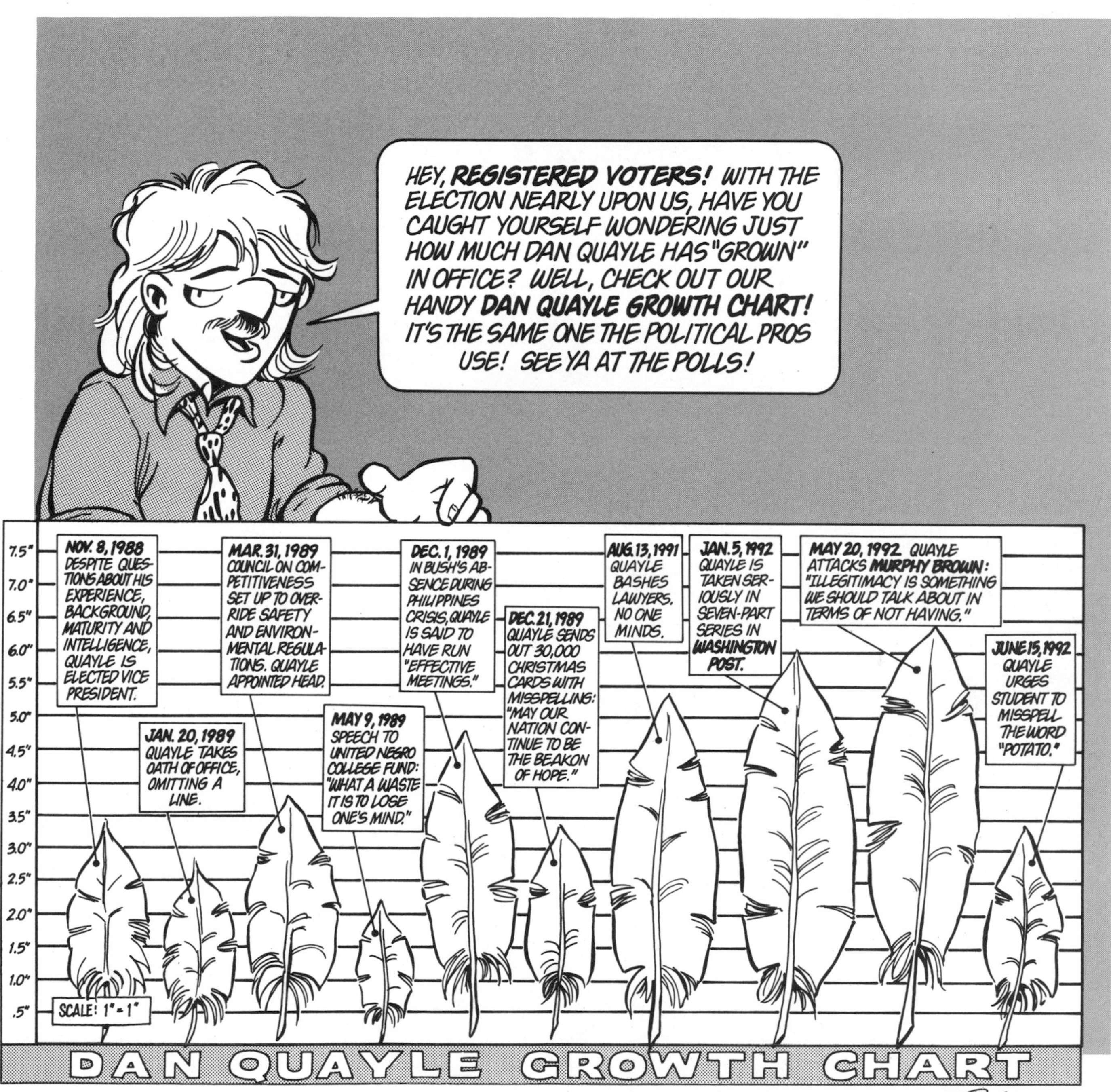
HEY, REGISTERED VOTERS! WITH THE ELECTION NEARLY UPON US, HAVE YOU CAUGHT YOURSELF WONDERING JUST HOW MUCH DAN QUAYLE HAS "GROWN" IN OFFICE? WELL, CHECK OUT OUR HANDY DAN QUAYLE GROWTH CHART! IT'S THE SAME ONE THE POLITICAL PROS USE! SEE YA AT THE POLLS!
7.5"
7.0"
6.5"
6.0"
5.5"
5.0"
4.5"
4.0"
3.5"
3.0"
2.5"
2.0"
1.5"
1.0"
.5"
NOV. 8, 1988 DESPITE QUESTIONS ABOUT HIS EXPERIENCE, BACKGROUND, MATURITY AND INTELLIGENCE, QUAYLE IS ELECTED VICE PRESIDENT.
JAN. 20, 1989 QUAYLE TAKES OATH OF OFFICE, OMITTING A LINE.
MAR. 31, 1989 COUNCIL ON COMPETITIVENESS SET UP TO OVERRIDE SAFETY AND ENVIRONMENTAL REGULATIONS. QUAYLE APPOINTED HEAD.
MAY 9, 1989 SPEECH TO UNITED NEGRO COLLEGE FUND: "WHAT A WASTE IT IS TO LOSE ONE'S MIND."
DEC. 1, 1989 IN BUSH'S ABSENCE DURING PHILIPPINES CRISIS, QUAYLE IS SAID TO HAVE RUN "EFFECTIVE MEETINGS."
DEC. 21, 1989 QUAYLE SENDS OUT 30,000 CHRISTMAS CARDS WITH MISSPELLING: "MAY OUR NATION CONTINUE TO BE THE BEAKON OF HOPE."
AUG. 13, 1991 QUAYLE BASHES LAWYERS. NO ONE MINDS.
JAN. 5, 1992 QUAYLE IS TAKEN SERIOUSLY IN SEVEN-PART SERIES IN WASHINGTON POST.
MAY 20, 1992 QUAYLE ATTACKS MURPHY BROWN: "ILLEGITIMACY IS SOMETHING WE SHOULD TALK ABOUT IN TERMS OF NOT HAVING."
JUNE 15, 1992 QUAYLE URGES STUDENT TO MISSPELL THE WORD "POTATO."
SCALE: 1" = 1"
DAN QUAYLE GROWTH CHART
GBTrudeau

MOSCOW-DECEMBER, 1969.
GOOD AFTERNOON, FIRST SECRETARY BREZHNEV!

GOOD AFTERNOON. I WOULD LIKE AN UPDATE ON CZECHOSLOVAKIA.

FIRST SECRETARY, WE HAVE CONTINUED TO TIGHTEN OUR GRIP. THE PARTY IS BEING PURGED TO ABOUT 65% OF MEMBERSHIP LEVEL BEFORE OUR INVASION!
GOOD, GOOD...

COMRADE SECRETARY? THERE IS AN AMERICAN COLLEGE STUDENT HERE TO SEE YOU.
WHAT? SHOW HIM IN! IMMEDIATELY!

MOSCOW-DECEMBER, 1969.
MR. BREZHNEV, I'LL COME RIGHT TO THE POINT...

I'M A YOUNG AMERICAN STUDENT, AND I'D LOVE TO ORGANIZE SOME ANTI-AMERICAN DEMONSTRATIONS ON FOREIGN SOIL!
I SEE. WOULD YOU BE WILLING TO BE A USEFUL IDIOT, A DUPE FOR THE KGB?

NO, NO, I COULDN'T DO THAT. I HAVE TO PROTECT MY POLITICAL VIABILITY...

BUT LOOK— LET'S SEE IF WE CAN'T FIND SOME MIDDLE GROUND.
HMM... THIS YOUNG MAN IS SLICK...

THEN IT'S SETTLED! I'LL ORGANIZE SOME ANTI-AMERICAN DEMONSTRATIONS WHILE MY COUNTRYMEN ARE DYING A HALF A WORLD AWAY!
GOOD, GOOD.

WELL, I BETTER BE GETTING BACK TO ENGLAND...
YOU ARE A REMARKABLE YOUNG MAN, AMERICAN STUDENT! I WOULD COMPARE YOU TO TOKYO ROSE OR HO CHI MINH!

WELL, I JUST HOPE NOBODY FINDS OUT I'VE BEEN HERE.
DON'T WORRY, WE'LL HAVE ONE OF OUR AGENTS IN THE STATE DEPARTMENT REMOVE THE VISA PAGES FROM YOUR PASSPORT FILE.
GOTCHA! HA, HA! GOTCHA!
GEORGE? GEORGE, WAKE UP...

IT WAS JUST A DREAM?
GEORGE, IT'S FOUR IN THE MORNING...

YEAH, BUT COULDA HAPPENED. COULDA. WON'T KNOW UNTIL HE LEVELS WITH... GETS THE FACTS OUT... NOT SAYING HE WAS IN A TREASON MODE, BUT COULDA HAPPENED. GOTTA TALK ABOUT IT.

COULD TURN THE CAMPAIGN AROUND. THE TRUST THING. AMERICAN PEOPLE COULD SAY, "HEY, FOUR MORE YEARS."

YOU'RE STILL DREAMING, GEORGE.
HEY, WORKS. GOTTA.

GOTTA GET SOME SLEEP... GOTTA BE IN... Z-CITY...

GOTTA... GET... ZZZZ!
HOLD IT! Y'ALL ARE KGB?
TOO LATE, MY LITTLE LOVEBIRD! WE HAVE PHOTOS!
GOT HIM! GOT HIM!
GEORGE, I'M MOVING INTO THE GUEST ROOM.

MR. PRESIDENT, WOULD YOU LIKE TO ATTACK GOVERNOR CLINTON AGAIN, OR SHALL WE GO TO OUR CALLERS?
LET'S GO TO THE CALLERS, LARRY...

...AND I'LL TELL YOU WHY. THE CALLERS ARE GOOD, DECENT AMERICANS. NOT SAYING THIS BIG-SPENDING DEMOCRAT GUY ISN'T. WOULDN'T DO THAT. NOT PRUDENT.

EVEN THOUGH, GOTTA SAY, TRIPS TO MOSCOW, MEETINGS, RAISES QUESTIONS. BUT, HEY, DON'T CRY FOR ME, LEONID. WAS THERE AN UNPATRIOTIC ANGLE? CAN'T SAY. WOULDN'T BE FAIR.

UM... OKAY. OUR FIRST CALLER IS...
KGB? TREASON? CAN'T SAY. DON'T HAVE THE FACTS.

MR. BUTTS! WHAT ARE YOU DOING HERE?
SAYING GOODBYE, SON—TO AN OLD FRIEND...

HIS NAME WAS WAYNE McLAREN. HE WAS ONE OF THE ORIGINAL MARLBORO MEN... DEAD AT 51! SOB!

OH, HEY, I READ ABOUT HIM. DIDN'T HE DIE OF LUNG CANCER, COMMONLY ASSOCIATED WITH SMOKING?
YES, IT WAS ANOTHER INCREDIBLY TRAGIC COINCIDENCE. AND IT'S GOING TO MAKE IT THAT MUCH TOUGHER TO REPLACE HIM.

IT'S GOING TO TAKE A RUGGED INDIVIDUALIST, SOMEONE WITH ENOUGH GRIT AND HEART TO STAND AGAINST THE WINDS OF CONVENTION!
WHAT DO YOU MEAN, MR. BUTTS?

GOSH...

MR. BUTTS, DO YOU SUPPOSE...
YOU? BUT YOU'RE JUST A LAD! OH, ALL RIGHT.

I'M NOT DOING THIS FOR MYSELF. THE PRESIDENCY IS A THANKLESS, DIRTY JOB, BUT I'M WILLING TO MAKE A WORLD-CLASS SACRIFICE IF THE PEOPLE BEG ME...
CLIK!

OUR ENTIRE PRIME-TIME SCHEDULE TONIGHT IS BEING PRE-EMPTED BY PART THREE OF "THE PEOPLE'S SERVANT"...
IT'S JUST THAT SIMPLE!
CLIK!

WORLD PEACE? STRICTLY ROUTINE. NO BIG DEAL.
JUST OPEN UP THE HOOD AND FIX IT! END OF STORY!
CLIK! CLIK!
©B Trudeau

WELCOME TO THE 24-HOUR PEROT CHANNEL!
YOU'RE GONNA HEAR A GIANT SUCKING SOUND, SEE?

CHUNKA!
E.D. 003
C.D. 08

CLINTON!
CHUNKA!

BUSH!
FLUSH!

FLUSH?
PEROT!
©B Trudeau

Mr. Editor: Please check boxes before publishing. Thanx!
CAN'T BELIEVE
❏ I
❏ SLICK WILLIE
❏ THE RUNT
WON...

WHO COULD HAVE PREDICTED THIS
❏ MIRACLE?
❏ DEBACLE?

GUESS THE ELECTION REALLY **WAS** ABOUT
❏ TRUST!
❏ CHANGE!
©B Trudeau

SURE AM LOOKING FORWARD TO FOUR MORE YEARS OF
❏ DOING NOTHING.
❏ DOING NOTHING.

Mr. Editor: Please check boxes before publishing. Thanx!
WONDER HOW THIS IRAN THING WILL PLAY OUT NOW THAT I'M ❑ RE-ELECTED. ❑ DEFEATED.

THIS DARN PAPER TRAIL STORY JUST STEAMS ME, MAKES ME WANT TO GO SEMI-BALLISTIC ON THIS ONE...

WHY DO PEOPLE WRITE SE-CRETS DOWN? CAN'T DO THAT! NOW EVERYONE WANTS TO KNOW WHERE I WAS ON THE LOOP THING!

WELL, THAT'S ONE STORY I'LL BE TAKING TO ❑ THE GRAVE. ❑ OPEN COURT.

HEY, KNEW IT WOULD HAPPEN. KNEW I'D BE ❑ HUMILIATED ❑ VINDICATED AT THE POLLS...

BEEN SUCH A SCREWY YEAR, TENSION CITY WITH THAT FREEZE CROWD OUT THERE COMIN' AT ME...

HELD OUR GROUND... BARBARA OUT THERE HUGGING THOSE AIDS BABIES, ME TAKIN' ON THAT ARKANSAS GUY!

MEANWHILE...
HEY, BILL CLINTON! WHERE YOU GOING NOW?
I'M GOING TO ❑ THE WHITE HOUSE! ❑ DISNEY-LAND!

SO WHAT'S THE ELECTION TELL US? CHANGE. GOTTA HAVE CHANGE. CHANGE IS GOOD. BUT PRUDENT CHANGE.

NUTTY OUT THERE... DON'T KNOW HOW THAT TAX-AND-SPEND GUY GOT AS MANY VOTES AS HE DID...

JUST HOPE HE'S AS GRACIOUS IN ❑ DEFEAT ❑ VICTORY AS I'VE BEEN IN ❑ VICTORY. ❑ DEFEAT.

HEY, GOVERNOR! WHAT'S JOB ONE— CLEANING UP THE MESS IN WASHINGTON OR HEALING WOUNDS?
WELL, I GUESS I'D LIKE IT ❑ BOTH WAYS. ❑ BOTH WAYS.

OKAY, IT'S NEARLY MID-NIGHT, AND GUESS WHO'S ON THE LINE — ROSS PEROT! MR. PEROT, CAN YOU HEAR ME?

CLEAR AS A BELL, SON. LET'S GO AT IT. LET'S DISCUSS THE ISSUES!
COOL. ISSUE ONE: NOW THE ELECTION IS OVER, WILL YOU BE RETURNING TO PRIVATE LIFE?

SON, IF I THOUGHT THE CANDIDATES HAD ADDRESSED THE ISSUES, I'D BE GONE. HISTORY. TOAST. I DON'T NEED THE AGGRAVATION.

I'VE HAD SOME OF MY PEOPLE — TOP PEOPLE — LOOK INTO IT, AND THEY TELL ME THAT THE C.I.A. CONTROLS EVERYTHING NOW ANYWAY. SO I DON'T NEED IT. NEVER DID. END OF STORY.

NOT THAT IT'S EVER BEEN UP TO ME. I DON'T CALL THE SHOTS. NEVER DID. NEVER HAPPENED. KNOW WHO MAKES THE FINAL DECISIONS?

UM... A TEAM OF WORLD-CLASS PSYCHIATRISTS?
JUST THAT SIMPLE. IT'S THEIR CALL. WHO?
©B Trudeau

BOOPSIE? SID! HOW'S THE GIG, BABE?
LOUSY! MY CHARACTER DOESN'T EVEN HAVE A NAME! I'M "SECOND BIMBO IN BAR"!

HEY, AT LEAST YOU'RE WORKING AGAIN. FIND A SITTER FOR THE KID?
YEAH, BUT SHE DIDN'T SHOW. B.D. HAD TO TAKE SAMANTHA TO WORK WITH HIM.

SAY WHAT?
I KNOW, I KNOW. I'M TRYING NOT TO THINK ABOUT IT.

WOULD YOU STEP OUT OF THE VEHICLE, PLEASE, SIR?
ASSUME THE POSITION, PUPPY-BREATH!

MAN! THAT PORSCHE IS ON A TEAR...
I'LL SAY!

HE'S CLOCKING 95! WONDER IF I SHOULD STOP HIM WITH SAM ON MY BACK...
GO FOR IT! NAIL THE TURKEY!

DANGER MOM AIN'T GONNA LIKE THIS,..
WHO CARES?
VROOM!

COULD WIPE OUT...
STOP WORRYING. I'VE GOT A ROLL BAR!
RR R RRRRR

QUALITY TIME ON HIGHWAY 1. NOTHING LIKE IT!
HOW'D SHE LIKE RIDING IN THE CRUISER?

THE CRUISER WAS IN THE SHOP. WE HAD TO USE THE MOTORCYCLE...
WHAT?

IT WAS GREAT! JUST AWESOME!
YOU TOOK THIS BABY ON A MOTORCYCLE? ARE YOU OUT OF YOUR MIND?

HEY, IT'S NOT LIKE I TOOK HER ON A HIGH-SPEED CHASE...
HOW LONG HAS SHE HAD THIS DIAPER SITUATION?
SINCE THE HIGH-SPEED CHASE!

B.D., TAKING SAM TO WORK WITH YOU IS **NOT** ACCEPTABLE! WE CAN'T GO ON LIKE THIS! WE NEED LIVE-IN HELP!

NO, WE DON'T THERE ARE PLENTY OF TEEN-AGE GIRLS WHO...
... FLAKE OUT! WHO DON'T SHOW UP! WHO CAN'T BE TRUSTED!

NOW, BOOPSIE...
B.D., THIS IS **IMPORTANT**! WE NEED **PROFESSIONAL HELP**!
©B'Trudeau

NO, I DIDN'T HEAR ANYTHING. WHY?
HMM... MUST HAVE BEEN THE T.V. ...

SON? ARE YOU PACKING? WHAT'S GOING ON?

TIME TO MOVE ON, POP. GAINFUL EMPLOY BECKONS.
YOU'VE GOT A **JOB**?

WELL, NOT YET. BUT I HAVE A GOOD FEELING ABOUT MY PROSPECTS.
YOU DO? WHY?
©B'Trudeau

ZONKER? BOOPSIE ON THE PHONE! SHE SOUNDS DISTRAUGHT.
CALL IT DESTINY. THANKS FOR EVERYTHING, DAD.

B.D., THERE'S NO WAY AROUND IT — WE **HAVE** TO HAVE A LIVE-IN!
OH, RIGHT. ON WHOSE SALARY?

DING DONG!
YOUR STARLET SALARY? MY ROOKIE CHIP SALARY? GET REAL!

WE JUST CAN'T AFFORD IT. END OF SUBJECT. WHO'S AT THE DOOR?
©B'Trudeau

IT IS I — MARY POPPINS!
NO! NO, NO, **NO!**

HI! O O o o
SO THIS IS THE LITTLE LADY!
FORGET IT, HARRIS. NO WAY YOU'RE LOOKING AFTER MY KID!

NOW, B.D., LET'S TRY TO KEEP AN OPEN MIND. AFTER ALL, I'M AN OLD HAND AT THIS...
HOW YOU FIGURE?

I TOOK CARE OF ALEX DOONESBURY FOR YEARS! I KNOW HOW TO COMMUNICATE WITH KIDS! I'M... I'M... WHAT'S THE WORD?
GBTrudeau

SIMPATICO!
THANK YOU.
FOR WHAT?

WE'RE IN LUCK! A BEACH FULL O' BABIES!
OH, BOY, OH, BOY...

NOW, SAMANTHA, I WANT YOU TO BE GOOD AS GOLD, OKAY? YOUR DADDY HAS A FEW MISGIVINGS ABOUT ME, AND WE HAVE TO SHOW HIM HE CAN TRUST US, GOT IT?
GOT IT!

GBTrudeau

CUTE BABY.
THANKS. COULD YOU LOOK AFTER HER FOR A WHILE?

SAM! STOP EATING THE SAND! PUT IT DOWN, SWEETHEART!

EDDIE! NO PULLING HAIR!
NO, NO, SAM!
SHAUNA! YOU'RE IN THE WAY, BABY!

EDDIE! AWAY FROM THE CAMERA!
STOP BOTHERING MISS STREISAND, SHAUNA!
GBTrudeau

CHILD CARE AT MALIBU.
SAM! GIVE MR. LETTERMAN HIS HAT BACK!

YOU KNOW, SAM, YOU'RE VERY LUCKY TO BE GROWING UP ON A BEACH SUCH AS THIS.

HERE YOU WILL HAVE THE CHANCE TO CHOOSE A MOST EXCELLENT LIFESTYLE — THAT OF THE SURFER. IT IS HERE THAT TRUE DUDES AND DUDESSES FIRST LEARN TO GO FOR IT.

THE SURF IS AN AWESOME TEACHER OF LIFE. IT CAN LIFT YOU TO UNIMAGINABLE JOY, AND JUST AS EASILY SEND YOU CRASHING INTO A CHASM OF DESPAIR. ALL THIS AWAITS YOU!

WHY WAIT? LET'S GO **NOW!**
BUT THERE'S A WARNING FLAG UP. OH, WELL.
©B Trudeau

I'M SORRY, BOOPSIE, ZONKER IS OUT OF THE QUESTION!
B.D., WHAT CHOICE DO WE HAVE?

WE BOTH HAVE TO WORK, AND WE HAVEN'T BEEN ABLE TO FIND AFFORDABLE, RELIABLE CHILD CARE **ANYWHERE!**

RELIABLE? YOU THINK ZONKER IS...
B.D., AT LEAST HE WON'T TAKE SAM ON A MOTORCYCLE! AT LEAST HE USES HIS **HEAD!**
©B Trudeau

HOW ABOUT THIS ONE?
NOT BIG ENOUGH!

I GOT A BAD FEELING ABOUT HIRING ZONKER, BOOPSIE, REALLY BAD...

HEY, C'MON, B.D., HE'S ALREADY IMPROVED OUR LIVES! WHEN WAS THE LAST TIME WE WENT OUT TO DINNER ALONE?

ISN'T IT NICE JUST KNOWING THAT OUR LITTLE GIRL IS BEING TUCKED SAFELY INTO BED BY SOMEONE WE KNOW AND TRUST?

HMM... MAYBE WE SHOULD BE HEADING IN...
NO, NO, ONE MORE, ONE MORE!
©B Trudeau

SORRY I'M LATE, WILLY...
THAT'S OKAY. DID YOU GET SOME?

SURE DID!
COOL! GOT ANY MATCHES?
SMOKING BEHIND THE BARN! DOESN'T THAT TAKE YOU BACK?

AN AMERICAN RITE OF PASSAGE, A CAMEO RIGHT OFF THE COVER OF THE OLD SATURDAY EVENING POST!

IT'S AN IMPORTANT PART OF OUR HERITAGE, AND WORTH REMEMBERING ON THIS, THE EVE OF THE GREAT AMERICAN SMOKE-OUT!

DO AMERICANS REALLY WANT THIS MARVELOUS ADOLESCENT RITUAL TO BECOME A THING OF THE PAST? HOW COULD THEY? LET'S LISTEN IN...

WOW... WICKED WEED, MAN!
OOPS! WRONG DRUG! OH, WELL, YOU GET THE POINT.
©B Trudeau

TODAY, TOP REPUBLICANS CONVENED ON CAPITOL HILL TO PICK THROUGH THE WRECKAGE OF THEIR COLLAPSED FORTUNES...

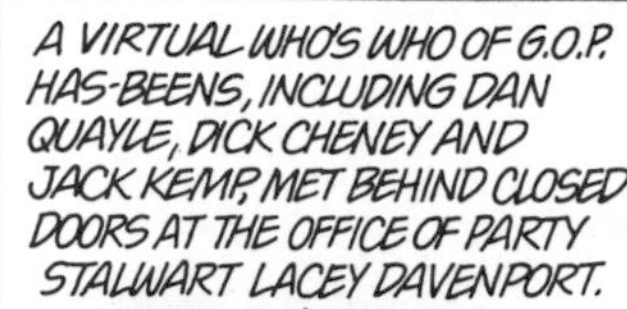
A VIRTUAL WHO'S WHO OF G.O.P. HAS-BEENS, INCLUDING DAN QUAYLE, DICK CHENEY AND JACK KEMP, MET BEHIND CLOSED DOORS AT THE OFFICE OF PARTY STALWART LACEY DAVENPORT.

TOPIC A? WHITHER THE G.O.P. IN THE FUTURE, AND EVEN MORE IMPORTANT, WHO WILL LEAD IT THERE?
©B Trudeau

I KNOW! I KNOW!
ANY OTHER SUGGESTIONS?

THE G.O.P. REGROUPS.
BEFORE WE BEGIN, I BELIEVE OUR OLD FRIEND PAT BUCHANAN HAS SOMETHING TO SAY...

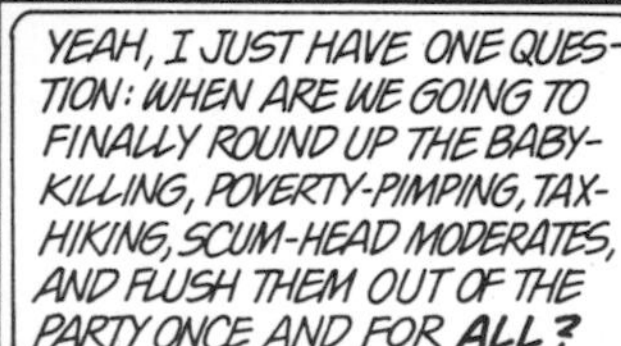
YEAH, I JUST HAVE ONE QUESTION: WHEN ARE WE GOING TO FINALLY ROUND UP THE BABY-KILLING, POVERTY-PIMPING, TAX-HIKING, SCUM-HEAD MODERATES, AND FLUSH THEM OUT OF THE PARTY ONCE AND FOR ALL?

WELL?
COULD SOMEONE GET PAT A HAMBURGER? WE'VE GOT WORK TO DO.
©B Trudeau

DEAR HEARTS, IT'S TIME FOR OUR GRAND OLD PARTY TO TAKE STOCK, TO ASK WHERE IT WENT ASTRAY, AND WHO WILL LEAD IT BACK!
OH, BOY, OH, BOY...

BUT FIRST, FOR THE RECORD, A WORD ABOUT LEADERSHIP PAST. I REFER, OF COURSE, TO THAT MOST FAITHFUL OF STEWARDS, GEORGE BUSH.

IN ALL MY YEARS, I CANNOT REMEMBER A DEFEATED PRESIDENT WHO HAS CONDUCTED HIMSELF WITH MORE PERSONAL DIGNITY AND GRACIOUSNESS. IN SO DOING, HE HAS ALLOWED THE HEALING TO BEGIN.
©B Trudeau

THERE IS NO GREATER BALM FOR...
WHO CARES? LET'S GET TO THE OTHER THING!

OKAY, BEFORE WE LOOK TO THE FUTURE, LET'S GO AROUND THE TABLE, AND FIND OUT WHERE WE WENT WRONG. CHARLIE, WOULD YOU LEAD US OFF?

SURE. THERE'S NO MYSTERY, LACEY—WE WERE TAKEN DOWN BY OUR OWN DIVISIVENESS.
VOTERS FELT EXCLUDED.

WE DIDN'T JUST FAIL TO FILL THE G.O.P.'s "BIG TENT"—WE **CLEARED** IT! AND THEN WE CLOSED THE BAR, INSULTED THE GUESTS, AND LOST THEIR CARS! NO **WONDER** THEY WENT ELSEWHERE!

I KNOW! LET'S USE A DIFFERENT METAPHOR! LIKE A JACUZZI OR SOMETHING!
WAIT YOUR TURN, DEAR. JACK?
YES, I'D LIKE TO FORMALLY DECLARE.

WELL, JACK RAISES A VALID POINT. DID WE REALLY GIVE SUPPLY-SIDE A FAIR CHANCE TO... WHY, MARILYN!
HI, HONEY! WHAT'S UP? YOU LOOK STEAMED!

I JUST WANT TO SAY THAT **YOU** PEOPLE LOST THIS ELECTION! DANNY DID HIS PART, BUT THE CAMPAIGN AND THE PARTY **BLEW IT!** YOU PEOPLE **OWE** HIM! YOU **OWE** HIM THE '96 NOMINATION!

I SEE.

WELL, THANK YOU, DEAR.
YEAH, THANKS, HONEY! I CAN TAKE IT FROM HERE!
WHAT ARE **YOU** STARING AT, BAKER?

WHO WILL LEAD THE G.O.P. INTO AN UNCERTAIN FUTURE? LOOK FOR FORMER SECRETARY OF STATE JAMES BAKER TO MAKE **HIS** CASE AT TODAY'S PARLEY...

WHILE BAKER CAN BE EXPECTED TO PRESENT HIMSELF AS A STATESMAN OF SOME DISTINCTION...

... HIS RIVALS WILL NO DOUBT SEEK TO DEFINE HIM IN SOMEWHAT DIFFERENT TERMS.

FAILED **HANDLER!** FAILED **HANDLER!**
DAN'S GOT A POINT, JIM, DEAR.

HOW'S HOME-WORK GOING TONIGHT, SPORT?
OKAY, I GUESS. DAD, DO YOU KNOW WHO CORTEZ WAS?

UM...CORTEZ? WELL, LEMME SEE... HE WAS... SOME SORT OF SAILOR OR SOMETHING...
NO, HE HELPED CONQUER MEXICO. HOW ABOUT CABOT?

CABOT... RINGS A BELL...HE WAS... LET'S SEE...
HE EXPLORED THE NORTH-EAST COAST OF AMERICA IN 1497 AND 1498...

SOME OF THE OTHER KEY EXPLORERS WERE MAGELLAN, WHO ALMOST MADE IT AROUND THE WORLD, AND VESPUCCI, WHO CHECKED OUT SOUTH AMERICA, AND DA GAMA, WHO SAILED TO INDIA!

VERY INTERESTING. WHY ARE YOU TELL-ING ME ALL THIS?
UM...I DUNNO. I GUESS I FEEL SORRY FOR YOU.

YOU WHAT?
YOU DON'T SEEM TO KNOW ANYTHING, DAD.

ED! YOU LOOK GREAT! HOW HAVE YOU BEEN?
NEVER BETTER. BUT WHY DO YOU ASK?

I JUST WONDERED.
WELL, I FIND THAT INTERESTING, SINCE IT'S THE FIRST TIME YOU'VE EVER ASKED ME.

I'VE BEEN BUSY PROTECTING MY WONDERFUL FAMILY FROM LIBYAN ASSASSINS.
IT'S TRUE. I'VE HAD MULTIPLE REPORTS TO THAT EFFECT!

A HIGHLY PLACED FRIEND OF MINE, SOMEONE THAT I TRUST, OKAY, IT'S ELVIS, BUT THAT'S A SECRET, ELVIS TOLD ME THAT THE CIA TOLD HIM ABOUT THE LIBYAN HIT SQUAD.

BUT ELVIS COULDN'T HAVE KNOWN! UNLESS... UNLESS HE WAS WIRE-TAPPING ME!
ELVIS INVOLVED IN WIRE-TAPPING? A LITTLE FAR-FETCHED, WOULDN'T YOU SAY?
WHO, THEN?

A REUNION OF PEROT VOTERS.
SIGH IF ONLY ROSS WERE HERE.
HE'D KNOW! SIMPLE AS THAT! END OF STORY!
GBTrudeau

WELL, IT'S NOW DAY 27 OF THE TRANSITION, CAMPERS, AND IT'S PRETTY QUIET OUT THERE...

THOUSANDS OF BABY BOOM DEMOCRATS STAND POISED TO HEED THE SUMMONS TO GLORY FROM ONE OF THEIR OWN!

RÉSUMÉS HAVE BEEN SENT, HINTS HAVE BEEN DROPPED NOTHING LEFT TO DO BUT WAIT FOR..."THE CALL"!

I'M NOT SURE STARING AT IT WILL HELP.
CAN'T HURT.
©B Trudeau

YOU REALLY SENT IN A RÉSUMÉ TO CLINTON?
UH-HUH. ME AND HALF THE OTHER STAFF LAWYERS ON THE HILL...

IT'S OUR TURN, RICK. WE'VE BEEN WAITING OUR WHOLE LIVES FOR A SHOT AT PUBLIC SERVICE. CLINTON'S ONE OF US, THE POINT MAN FOR AN ENTIRE GENERATION!

AND SO YOU'RE GOING TO SIT THERE BY THE PHONE, WAITING FOR HIS CALL?
RICK, IF HE CALLS, IT'LL BE THE CULMINATION OF MY LIFE! AND HE WILL CALL! I KNOW HE'LL CALL!
©B Trudeau

SOUNDS LIKE HIGH SCHOOL.
SORT OF. ONLY I'VE GOT MY HAIR RESOLVED.

RICK, THEY HAVE TO GIVE ME A LOOK! IT'S TRUE I DON'T HAVE MUCH POLICY EXPERIENCE, BUT I DID A LOT OF THE SPADE WORK ON THE FAMILY LEAVE BILL!

ALBEIT UNDER THE PATRONAGE OF A WELL-KNOWN REPUBLICAN.
A MODERATE REPUBLICAN! LACEY'S PRACTICALLY A DEMOCRAT!

DAMMIT, I'M THE RIGHT AGE!
AND YOU DON'T LOOK IT, EITHER.
EARTH IN THE BALANCE
©B Trudeau

HI, JOANIE. GET THE CALL YET?

NOPE. DID YOU, LYNN?
AFRAID NOT. I CAN'T UNDERSTAND IT.

WERE THERE ANY MAJOR APPOINTMENTS FROM THE HILL TODAY?
ONE. TREASURY UNDERSECRETARY. THEY PICKED LOWELL FROM ACCOUNTING.
©B Trudeau

LOWELL FROM ACCOUNTING?
APPARENTLY, HE GAVE ONE HELL OF AN INTERVIEW.

SIGH...

BRRING!

I'M READY TO SERVE! I MEAN, HELLO?
YEAH, GIMME ROCKY! THAT YOU, ROCKY?
©B Trudeau

JUST A MINUTE, SIR. I'LL SEE IF I CAN FIND HER.
WHO'S IT FOR?

JOANIE. IT'S THE CALL.
THE CALL?

JOANIE GOT THE CALL?
SHE GOT THE CALL.
©B Trudeau

JOANIE? I HATE YOU.
IS IT THE CALL? I GOT THE CALL?

HEY, MIKE, CHECK THIS OUT...
WHAT?

IT'S ALEX. SHE'S PULLED OUT YOUR BOOKS AGAIN.
I KNOW...

SHE LIKES MY ART BOOKS BEST. SHE SEEMS PARTICU-LARLY TAKEN WITH DAUMIER.

HEE, HEE!
HONEY? WHATCHA LOOKING AT?

IT'S A FUNNY BOOK, MOMMY. IT HAS PIC-TURES OF FUNNY PEOPLE.
SEE? DAUMIER AGAIN.

THE METAL COVERS ARE FUNNY, TOO.
THE WHAT?
UH-OH...

HI, LYNN, IT'S RICK. IS JOANIE IN THE OFFICE?
YOU DIDN'T HEAR? SHE GOT THE CALL!

THE CALL?
FROM THE CLINTONIANS! SHE JUST WENT OVER FOR HER INTERVIEW!

SHE HAS TO TAKE A STANDARDIZED CLINTON APTITUDE TEST. THEY CALL IT THE CAT SCAN.
©B Trudeau

WHO'S THE BASS PLAYER FOR THE GRATEFUL DEAD?
RIGHT. TAKE YOUR TIME.

MS. CAUCUS, THESE ARE JUST ROUTINE QUESTIONS FROM OUR STANDARDIZED CLINTON APTITUDE TEST...

WE CALL IT OUR CAT SCAN, BECAUSE IT HELPS US UNDERSTAND WHAT'S GOING ON IN YOUR HEAD.
GREAT.

THE FIRST SECTION ISN'T CRITICAL, BUT IT DOES HELP US LOCATE YOU CULTURALLY, OKAY? HERE WE GO...
PLEASE, GOD, NO MORE ROCK BAND QUESTIONS.
©B Trudeau

WHERE DID RICHARD PETTY LAST FLAME OUT?
BETTER FAKE IT.
WOODSTOCK?

UM... SORRY, I DON'T KNOW OTIS REDDING'S BIRTHPLACE.
NO PROBLEM. IT'S JUST A WARM-UP QUESTION.

NOW THEN, LET'S FIND OUT A LITTLE ABOUT YOUR SENSE OF GENERATIONAL IDENTITY, SHALL WE?
UM... OKAY.

PLEASE ANSWER THE FOLLOWING QUESTION. HAVING A PRESIDENT ROUGHLY YOUR OWN AGE MAKES YOU FEEL HOW? A) OLD; B) INADEQUATE; C) LIKE A TOTAL FAILURE.

©B Trudeau
THOSE ARE THE ONLY CHOICES?
IF YOU'RE HONEST.

ALL RIGHT, MS. CAUCUS, LET'S RUN THROUGH A FEW HYPOTHETICAL SITUATIONS YOU MIGHT ENCOUNTER IF YOU WERE TO JOIN OUR TEAM.
FINE.

OKAY, LET'S SAY YOU'RE WORKING NIGHT DUTY AT THE NEW NATIONAL ECONOMIC COUNCIL. SAY THE GERMAN STOCK MARKET SUDDENLY COLLAPSES.

IT'S 3:30 A.M. — WHAT DO YOU DO? A) WAKE UP THE SECRETARY OF THE TREASURY; B) WAKE UP THE SECRETARY OF STATE...
©B Trudeau

c) INTERRUPT THE PRESIDENT'S CARD GAME.
THAT'S IT!

OKAY, MS. CAUCUS, A COUPLE MORE QUESTIONS, AND WE'LL HAVE YOU OUT OF HERE...

SAY YOU'RE WORKING ON DOMESTIC POLICY. THE PRESIDENT ASKS YOU TO RETOOL THE FAMILY LEAVE BILL SO IT'S LESS COSTLY TO BUSINESS.

BUT AS YOU'RE LEAVING THE OVAL OFFICE, HILLARY TAKES YOU ASIDE AND TELLS YOU TO LEAVE THE BILL ALONE. WHAT DO YOU DO?
©B Trudeau

UM...
AGAIN, TAKE YOUR TIME. LOTS OF IT.

ONLY ONE QUESTION LEFT, MS. CAUCUS — A TWO-PARTER...

1. WHAT DID YOU DO WITH YOUR LIFE WHILE WAITING FOR YOUR GENERATION TO COME TO POWER?

I DEDICATED MYSELF TO SOLVING COMPLICATED, REAL-WORLD PROBLEMS, TRYING TO LEAD A LIFE OF PURPOSE AND MEANING IN PREPARATION FOR THE CHANCE TO SERVE.
©B Trudeau

2. WHAT DID YOU **REALLY** DO?
I WAS AFRAID OF THAT...

UM... HOW'D IT GO, BABE?

COMPLETE DISASTER. I DIDN'T KNOW ANY OF THE CULTURAL STUFF, AND I COULDN'T STOP STAMMERING! WORST INTERVIEW I'VE **EVER** HAD!

WHO AM I KIDDING? THEY'LL NEVER HIRE ME! NOT WHEN THEY CAN HAVE THEIR PICK OF THE BRIGHTEST, MOST EXPERIENCED HANDS IN THE COUNTRY!
©B Trudeau

NEXT!
ABOUT TIME!
GOOD LUCK, SIR.

NO WAY I'M GETTING A JOB, RICK. THE COMPETITION'S TOO INTENSE.

OH, I DON'T KNOW ABOUT THAT. I SAW OUR OLD FRIEND DUKE IN THE WAITING ROOM.

DUKE? MY GOD, WOULD THEY REALLY GIVE HIM ANOTHER POSTING?
ANYTHING'S POSSIBLE. HE DOES HAVE A KNACK FOR LANDING ON HIS FEET.

HOW MUCH FOR WHAT, MR. DUKE?
BERMUDA. OR BARBADOS. WE TALKING FOUR FIGURES?
©B Trudeau

ANY WORD TODAY?
NOPE...

BRIINGG!
I FIGURE I ALMOST CERTAINLY TALKED MY WAY OUT OF A JOB YESTERDAY...

...BUT FOR SOME REASON I HAVEN'T GIVEN UP HOPE. I HAVE AN ABSURDLY GOOD FEELING ABOUT MY CHANCES.

FBI, MA'AM. BACKGROUND CHECK.
YESSS!
©B Trudeau

RICK! GUESS WHO'S HERE! THE FBI! I'M BEING INVESTIGATED!

ISN'T THAT GREAT? IT'S A BACKGROUND CHECK! ME, JOANIE CAUCUS, IS HAVING HER BACKGROUND CHECKED!

I CAN'T BELIEVE IT! I WAS SURE I BLEW THE INTERVIEW! AND THEN I OPEN MY DOOR AND WOW — AN FBI AGENT!
THAT'S GREAT, BABE. CONGRATULATIONS!

I CANNOT BELIEVE YOU'RE HERE!
I FEEL LIKE ED McMAHON.
I'LL GET THE CAMERA!

SO WHERE WOULD YOU LIKE TO START, INSPECTOR?
WELL, FIRST I NEED A LITTLE PERSONAL DATA, MA'AM. YOU WERE MARRIED ONCE BEFORE, CORRECT?
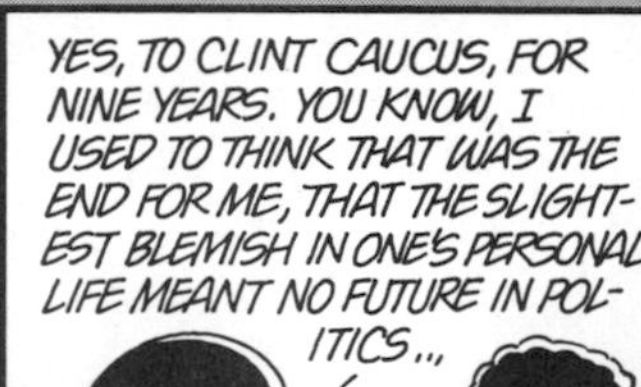
YES, TO CLINT CAUCUS, FOR NINE YEARS. YOU KNOW, I USED TO THINK THAT WAS THE END FOR ME, THAT THE SLIGHTEST BLEMISH IN ONE'S PERSONAL LIFE MEANT NO FUTURE IN POLITICS...

IRONIC, ISN'T IT?
I HOPE NOT. IT'S AGAINST PROCEDURE TO USE IRONY IN A BUREAU REPORT.

REALLY? HOW COME?
IT MESSES UP THE COMPUTERS. IS "CAUCUS" HIS REAL NAME OR IRONIC?

DON'T TAKE OFFENSE AT ANY OF THESE QUESTIONS, MA'AM, THEY'RE STRICTLY ROUTINE. FIRST OF ALL, HAVE YOU EVER USED ILLEGAL DRUGS?

WELL, YES, ONCE. BUT LIKE CLINTON, I DIDN'T INHALE! HA, HA!

HEE...

IT WAS A JOKE. I'M NERVOUS. YOU DON'T NEED TO PUT IT IN...
"SUBJECT ENJOYS JOKES AT PRESIDENT-ELECT'S EXPENSE."

WHAT'S HAPPENIN', Z-MAN?

RAYMOND! COOL TO SEE YOU!
WHAT'S UP WITH THE HAT?

THE HAT? IT'S PROTECTION FROM THE SUN, SON!
NO, I MEAN THE "X."

OH, THAT. I DUNNO, I SAW IT ON THE STREET, AND I JUST TOOK TO IT, HAD TO HAVE ONE.
WHY?

IT'S WHO I AM. I IDENTIFY WITH IT. LEAST, HALF OF ME DOES.
YO, ZONK— YOU KNOW WHAT "X" STANDS FOR?
GB Trudeau

UM...SURE. THE FAMOUS SEX CHROMOSOME, RIGHT?
ZONKER! THERE'S A CHILD PRESENT!

MOMS! DADS! BEEN TOO BUSY TO BUY SIS OR JUNIOR A CHRISTMAS PRESENT? NOT TO WORRY — SANTA'S HERE TO BAIL YOU OUT! JUST CUT OUT OUR SPECIAL PAPER DOLL, MOUNT IT ON CARDBOARD, AND "SHRINK-WRAP" IT WITH SARAN WRAP! WITH ITS AUTHENTIC-LOOKING BAR CODE AND PRICE TAG, NO ONE WILL BE THE WISER! SO RELAX — AND HAVE A COOL YULE!
ACME TOY COMPANY
FULLY ACCESSORIZED DUDE!
ZONKER CUT-OUT
• 100% real paper • Lots of colors
• Non-violent • Mildly amusing
9.99
X
SPF 2
SPF 10
SPF 30
GEORGE HAMILTON COCOA BUTTER OPEN
PROOF OF PURCHASE
0 76281 63920 8
©B Trudeau

A HOLIDAY REUNION.
HEY, BUTTSIE!
JOEY! JOEY CAMEL!

WE'VE MISSED YOU, STRANGER! HOW COME YOU NEVER COME BACK TO THE NEIGHBORHOOD, MR. BIG SHOT INDUSTRY ICON?
HEE, HEE...

BEEN TAKING CARE OF BUSINESS, BUTTSIE! TALKIN' TO THE KIDS, MOVIN' MILLIONS OF THEM INTO OUR COLUMN! AND DOIN' IT WITH JUST PRINT ADS!

IF I WERE ANIMATED, I'D OWN THIS GENERATION! OWN IT!
YIKES! YOU'RE SCARY, JOE! YOU'RE SCARIN' ME HERE!

SO, JOSEPH! HOME FOR THE HOLIDAYS?
YEAH. I NEED A BREAK. I'M COMING OFF ANOTHER MONSTER YEAR...

I GOT A 90% RECOGNITION FACTOR WITH SIX-YEAR-OLDS NOW! MY SHARE OF THE ILLEGAL CHILDREN'S MARKET HAS GONE FROM 1% TO 30%! I'M TAKING IN $500 MILLION IN SALES TO MINORS...

JOEY... JOEY...
WHAT?

IT'S ME, BUTTSIE! YOU DON'T HAVE TO IMPRESS ME!
SORRY, MAN. COMING BACK TO THE HOOD ALWAYS MAKES ME INSECURE...

WHAT A YEAR! ONE BRUTAL PRINT AD CAMPAIGN AFTER ANOTHER! PHOTO SHOOTS, PROMOTIONAL EVENTS, MERCHANDISING — IT NEVER ENDS!

KNOW WHY I DO IT? THE KIDS! THE THOUSANDS OF YOUNGSTERS WHO BECOME ADDICTED TO OUR PRODUCT EVERY DAY!
THEY MAKE IT ALL WORTH WHILE!

KNOW WHAT ONE LITTLE GIRL TOLD ME? SHE TOLD ME SHE LIKED SMOKING BECAUSE IT MADE HER FEEL "GROWN-UPPY".

"GROWN-UPPY"? THAT'S ADORABLE!
ISN'T IT? YOU SHOULD SEE HER FUMBLE WITH THE LIGHTER.

JOEY, WHAT'S YOUR SE-CRET? HOW DID YOU TURN A LOSER LIKE CAMEL INTO **THE** HOT BUTT?

ATTITUDE, MOSTLY. YOUR ENTRY-LEVEL SMOKER IS VERY CONCERNED WITH BEING COOL, SO I HAD TO POSITION THE PRODUCT AS THE CHILLIEST, DOWNEST, BADDEST STICK IN TOWN!

AS FOR THE ESTABLISHED SMOKERS, I GUESS THEY JUST IDENTIFY WITH A CAMEL.
GB Trudeau

THEY DO?
SURE! FOUL BREATH, BROWN TEETH, SMELLY HAIR—YOU NAME IT!

YOU KNOW, BUTTSIE, EVEN **I'M** AMAZED BY MY POPULARITY. I DON'T QUITE GET IT.
HERE COMES A TEEN-LET'S ASK HIM ABOUT IT...

HEY, KID. YOU REC-OGNIZE THIS MUG?
ARE YOU KID-DING? HE'S **JOE CAMEL!** HE'S MY HERO, A **MAJOR** ROLE MODEL!

ROLE MODEL? REALLY?
BETTER BELIEVE IT!
GB Trudeau

YOU REALIZE HE'S NOT REAL? THAT HE'S A CAR-TOON CHARACTER?
BIG DEAL. SO AM I.

HERE'S TO YOU, BIG GUY! YOU'RE THE KILLER, THE BADDEST OF THE BAD!
HEE, HEE!

THOUGH TO BE HONEST, I'M A LITTLE SUR-PRISED TO SEE YOU HERE!

WHAT, A GUY CAN'T HAVE A QUICK POP WHEN HE'S OFF-DUTY?
NO, I'M TALKING COPY-RIGHT INFRINGE-MENT! YOU'RE NOT ACTUALLY A CHAR-ACTER IN THIS STRIP!
WHAT STRIP?
WHAT?
GB Trudeau

MAIL, MAIL, MAIL! YOU SEND IT, WE IGNORE IT!
U.S.M

UNTIL TODAY, THAT IS! TIME FOR OUR YEAR-END MAILBAG, IN WHICH WE ANSWER YOUR QUESTIONS ABOUT THIS QUALITY FEATURE!

WHOA! CHECK OUT THIS LETTER, MIKE! THE GUY SENT MONEY!
MONEY?

"DEAR ZONKER: COULD YOU MENTION MY NAME IN THE STRIP? SINCERELY, BARRY SVIGALS."
HEY! WE DON'T DO THAT KIND OF THING! NICE TRY, BARRY SVIGALS!

OKAY, LET'S CHECK OUT ANOTHER READER LETTER FROM THE OL' MAIL SILO! "DEAR GUYS: HOW WILL THE NEW NORTH AMERICAN TRADE AGREEMENT AFFECT YOU?"

"ARE THERE ANY PLANS TO RELOCATE THE STRIP? JUST CURIOUS. SINCERELY, N.K., SANTA FE, NEW MEXICO."

UM... WELL, N.K., THAT'S SORT OF AN AWKWARD ONE...
YOU SAID IT.

ACTUALLY, THE STRIP'S BEEN PRODUCED IN GUATEMALA SINCE 1979.
BUT ALL THE IDEAS ARE AMERICAN! EVERY ONE!

HERE'S A ROUGH ONE, ZONKER! IT COMES TO US FROM J.M. OF CHEVY CHASE. "DEAR SIR: WHY DON'T YOU TURN OVER THE ILLUSTRATION TO SOMEONE WITH SOME DRAWING SKILLS?"

WELL, J.M., WHAT YOUR HURTFUL LETTER DOESN'T ACKNOWLEDGE IS HOW FAR THIS FEATURE HAS COME! TAKE A LOOK AT THE FIRST DAY OF SYNDICATION!

HI THERE! MY NAME'S MIKE DOONESBURY. I HAIL FROM TULSA, OKLAHOMA AND WOMEN ADORE ME! GLAD TO MEET YOU, ROOMIE!

SO YOU SEE, IT COULD BE WORSE...
I DUNNO, I SORT OF PREFER THAT PERIOD.

HERE'S ANOTHER ONE ALONG THE SAME LINES, MIKE! C.P. OF NEW HAVEN WRITES: "I HEARD A RUMOR YOU USE A GHOST ARTIST. MY ADVICE: FIRE THIS PERSON AT ONCE!"

AND HERE'S ONE MORE, Z! IT'S FROM W.M. OF MILTON. "DEAR SIR: WHO DRAWS THOSE UGLY CHARACTERS? MIKE IS ESPECIALLY POORLY DRAWN!"

>SIGH< ... THINK WE SHOULD 'FESS UP?
I GUESS SO.

IT'S NOT THE DRAWING, FOLKS. WE REALLY LOOK LIKE THIS.
WE DON'T GET ANY BETTER.
©B Trudeau

MIKE, THIS PROVOCATIVE QUERY COMES TO US FROM J.W. IN BOSTON. "DEAR ZONK: HOW COME THERE ARE SO FEW AFRICAN-AMERICANS IN YOUR FEATURE?"

WELL, ACTUALLY, J.W., THERE'VE BEEN QUITE A FEW BLACKS IN THE STRIP THROUGH THE YEARS, INCLUDING...
THOR...
GINNY...
CLYDE...

PETIT-POIS...
JEANIE...
PLUS SOME DYNAMIC NEWCOMERS...
RAY...
MAY...
...AND DES!

HERE'S AN INTERESTING ONE, Z! "DEAR SIR: HOW COME YOU'VE GOT SO MANY BLACK CHARACTERS?"
BEATS ME. PROBABLY TO KEEP THEM FROM GOING TO OTHER STRIPS.
©B Trudeau

"DEAR GUYS: HOW COME WE DON'T SEE ANY POSITIVE IMAGES OF LATINOS IN YOUR FEATURE? G.C., SANTA FE."
YO, G.C., WHERE HAVE YOU BEEN? SAY HELLO TO OUR REGULAR LATINO CAST MEMBERS!

PROFESSOR HENRY GOMEZ...
JUDGE MARIA RAMIREZ...
MAYOR EDDIE TORRES...
TEEN IDOL MIKE MESA...
DR. CONSUELA SANTANA...
...AMONG MANY OTHERS!

THAT'S ODD. I'VE NEVER LAID EYES ON EVEN ONE OF THESE...
SHHH! IT'S LICENSE RENEWAL TIME.
©B Trudeau

BOYS! GIRLS! CHECK IT OUT!

THIS STORE SELLS CIGARETTES TO MINORS!

A Mr. Butts SALUTE!

HERE'S A PROVOCATIVE LETTER, Z! IT COMES TO US FROM R.C. IN NEW YORK CITY...
WHAT'S UP WITH R.C.?

"DEAR DUDES: ENOUGH WITH THE LETTERS ALREADY. WHEN ARE YOU GOING TO RETURN TO THE ACTION?"
WHOA! POINT WELL TAKEN, R.C.! WE'RE ON IT!

LET'S CATCH UP ON RAY'S STORY, OKAY? WHEN LAST WE CHECKED IN WITH THE ROOKIE STATE TROOPER, HE HAD HIS HANDS FULL WITH DES, THE TEEN-AGE SON OF MAY, HIS NEW LADY.

YO, I HATE THIS STORY, MAN.
WHAT STORY? IS YOUR MAMA HOME?
©B. Trudeau

HEY, BABY, YOU READY?
ALMOST, RAY! WHY DON'T YOU AND DES GET TO KNOW EACH OTHER A LITTLE BETTER?

WHY? 'CAUSE DES DON'T NEED NO POLICE ANYWHERE NEAR HIS FACE!
HEY, LIGHTEN UP, LITTLE BRO. YOU DON'T EVEN KNOW ME.

DON'T NEED TO KNOW YOU, CHIPPER! 'SIDES, I'M BUSY, MAN. I'M WORKIN' ON MY FUTURE.
WHAT FUTURE'S THAT, DES?

I'M TRYING TO DECIDE WHAT GANG TO JOIN.
YO, GET THE FACTS. ASK ABOUT FATALITY RATES.
RAY! THAT'S NOT HELPFUL!
©B. Trudeau

SO, DES—HOW'S EVERYTHING AT SCHOOL?
GOOD, MAN. THE METAL DETECTOR'S BROKE.

DES, WHAT'S UP WITH ALL THE TOUGH-GUY STUFF? YOU THINK YOU GOTTA BE TEN SHADES OF BAD TO MAKE YOUR WAY IN THE WORLD? WRONG, LITTLE BRO...

I WANT YOU TO COME DOWN TO TROOP HEADQUARTERS WITH ME, MEET SOME OF THE BROTHERS, SEE WHAT IT MEANS TO STEP UP TO SOME REAL RESPONSIBILITY, OKAY?
©B. Trudeau

YO, MAMA! HE'S PULLIN' THAT ROLE-MODEL CRAP AGAIN!
CUT IT OUT, RAY! WHY CAN'T YOU TWO GET ALONG?

YOU SEE "MALCOLM X" YET, DES?
'COURSE I HAVE, FOOL.

WHAT DID YOU THINK?
I THINK MY MAN SPIKE GOT BROTHER MALCOLM COLD, EVEN IF SOME THINGS ABOUT X'S PAST DIDN'T QUITE GO DOWN THE WAY HE SAYS. ALSO, SPIKE DIDN'T SHOW ENOUGH RESPECT FOR THE HEAVY-LIFTIN' BROTHERS LIKE KING, ABERNATHY AND YOUNG.

©B Trudeau

DAMN. I WAS GETTING ALL SET TO PATRONIZE YOU.
YO, I GOT TEACHERS FOR THAT, MAN.

I'M REALLY SORRY ABOUT DES, RAY. HE'S JUST BEEN SO OUT OF CONTROL LATELY...
DON'T WORRY ABOUT ME AND DES, MAY. I CAN HANDLE HIS ACT.

THAT'S WHAT THE LAST GUY I DATED SAID. HE TOLD ME HE LOVED KIDS...

NEXT THING I KNOW, HE'S SAYING, "IT'S EITHER HIM OR ME."
WICKED. HOW LONG HAD YOU BEEN DATING?

ABOUT AN HOUR AND A HALF.
WON'T HAPPEN TO ME. 'COURSE, I'M ARMED.
©B Trudeau

DES HAS BEEN LIKE THIS FOR ALMOST TWO YEARS, RAY, EVER SINCE HIS FATHER AND I SPLIT.
DOES DES EVER SEE HIS FATHER?

NOT MUCH. HE GOT A NEW JOB WITH HIS COMPANY IN SEATTLE. SO IT'S JUST HOLIDAYS MOSTLY...

...FOR WHICH I'M ROYALLY PUNISHED WITH NON-STOP ATTITUDE.
I MIGHT HAVE SEEN A LITTLE OF THAT SIDE MYSELF.
©B Trudeau

YO, NOW HE'S DISSING ME BEHIND MY BACK! WHO COMES UP WITH THIS STUFF?
ORDINARY PEOPLE, SON. WE USE FOCUS GROUPS.

SORRY TO INTERRUPT FOLKS, BUT WE JUST GOT ANOTHER **FASCINATING** LETTER IN!
THWAP!

LISTEN TO THIS: "DEAR GUYS, DO YOU EVER CUT AWAY FROM AN ONGOING STORY TO COMMENT ON A BREAKING NEWS EVENT? SINCERELY, M.T., LONG BEACH."

DEAR M.T. : NO WAY! WE WOULD **NEVER** COMPROMISE THE PACING AND STRUCTURE OF A PLOT LINE JUST TO COMMENT ON SOME TOPICAL EVENT, UNLESS, OF COURSE, IT WERE UNIQUELY OUTRAGEOUS...

COVER-UP? WHAT COVER-UP?
©B Trudeau

HATE PACKING... GOTTA DO IT. BUT HATE IT!

OKAY, WHERE IS IT?... LEFT IT RIGHT HERE IN MY OFFICE...

DAMN... DON'T WANNA LEAVE WITHOUT IT...
©B Trudeau

BAR! YOU SEEN MY HONOR?
UM... NO. NOT SINCE CHRISTMAS EVE.

MR. PRESIDENT, WE'RE TAKING A LOT OF HITS OVER THE MISSING PAGES OF YOUR DIARY...

WE NEED TO DEVELOP A PLAUSIBLE RATIONALE FOR WHY WE'VE WITHHELD KEY SECTIONS FROM THE SPECIAL PROSECUTOR.

HOW ABOUT IF WE SAY, "HEY, GOTTA PUT THOSE PAGES BEHIND US, GOTTA MOVE ON."
BUT THAT DOESN'T EXPLAIN WHY THEY'RE MISSING.

THE DOG ATE THEM?
NO, MILLIE'S A WRITER HERSELF. NO ONE'D BELIEVE IT.
©B Trudeau

SIR, WE'VE HAD ANOTHER REQUEST FROM JUDGE WALSH FOR...
NOT GONNA DO IT. WON'T. GIVEN HIM, THAT PROSECUTING GUY, ALL HE NEEDS TO GO, "HEY, BUSH, OUT OF LOOP!"

LISTEN TO THESE EXCERPTS FROM MY DIARY: "NOV. 24, 1987. WENT TO MEETING, COVER-UP THING DISCUSSED, BUT WASN'T PAYING ATTENTION. SAME AS IF NOT REALLY THERE."

AND HOW ABOUT THIS — "NOV. 25, 1987. JUST REMEMBERED I HEARD NOTHING AT JAN. 7, 1986, MEETING WHEN REAGAN TOLD US HE FAVORED ARMS FOR HOSTAGES..."

"... MUST HAVE BEEN OUT TAKING A WHIZ OR SOMETHING."
WOW! ENOUGH SAID, SIR!
GB Trudeau

AMONG THE MANY QUESTIONS THAT MR. BUSH'S CHRISTMAS COVER-UP PROVOKES ARE THESE: DID THE PRESIDENT PARDON MR. WEINBERGER TO AVOID HAVING TO TESTIFY ABOUT HIS **OWN** ROLE IN IRANGATE?

AND WHY DID MR. BUSH WAIT YEARS TO PRODUCE NOTES HE CLAIMED HE NEVER HAD? WHY DO ENTIRE SECTIONS APPEAR TO BE MISSING? WERE THE TRANSCRIPTS "EDITED" BEFORE THEY WERE TURNED OVER?

WHETHER OR NOT THESE QUESTIONS ARE EVER FULLY ANSWERED, ONE THING HAS NOW BECOME CLEAR: GEORGE BUSH WILL BE REMEMBERED AS THE PRESIDENT WHO COVERED UP THE IRANGATE SCANDAL...
GB Trudeau

...LONG AFTER HIS MILITARY ADVENTURES HAVE BEEN FORGOTTEN!
WHAT ABOUT MY WARS? WHAT ABOUT MY WARS?

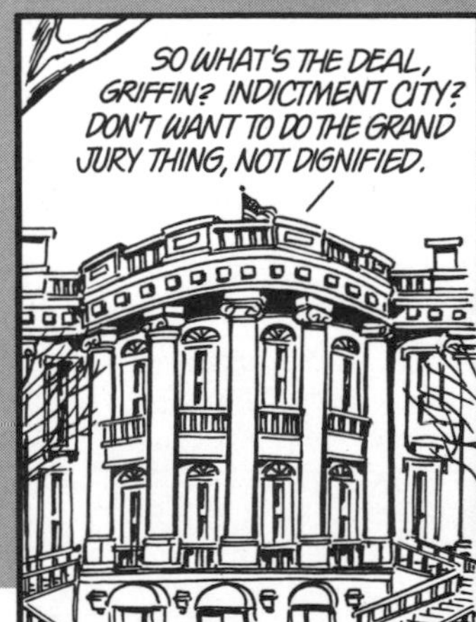
SO WHAT'S THE DEAL, GRIFFIN? INDICTMENT CITY? DON'T WANT TO DO THE GRAND JURY THING, NOT DIGNIFIED.

YOU MAY NOT HAVE ANY CHOICE, SIR. YOU'RE BEING INVESTIGATED BY THE SPECIAL PROSECUTOR FOR ILLEGALLY WITHHOLDING DOCUMENTS. HE COULD MAKE IT STICK...

SIGH... MAYBE I SHOULD JUST PARDON MYSELF. CONSTITUTION ALLOWS IT. COULD BE THE WAY TO GO...
GB Trudeau

YES! **YES!** PLEASE! **PLEEEASE!**
NOW, NOW, DON'T GET GREEDY. HE'S DONE ENOUGH FOR US.

DAD-O-RAMA! STILL IN BED?
HMPFF...

C'MON! SHAKE A LEG! GET A MOVE ON! GET THE LEAD OUT OF YOUR P.J.s!
OKAY, OKAY... I'M UP...

WHAT AM I GOING TO DO WITH YOU, DADDY! YOU'RE NEVER GOING TO FIND A JOB AT THIS RATE! YOU GOTTA GET CRACKING!

YOU KNOW SOMETHING, SWEETHEART? WHEN YOU'RE RIGHT, YOU'RE RIGHT! THINGS ARE GOING TO CHANGE AROUND HERE...

... STARTING TODAY! I'M NOT WASTING ONE MORE MINUTE! I'M GOING TO HIT THE SHOWERS, AND THEN HIT THE STREET! I'M TAKING BACK MY SELF-RESPECT!

DINNER!
GOTTA GO. NICE SPEECH, THOUGH, DAD.
UM... THANKS.
©B Trudeau

JUSTICE? YOU'RE GOING TO JUSTICE?
YOU'RE NOT ANGRY, LACEY?

ANGRY? HEAVENS NO, DEAR! WHY WOULD I BE ANGRY? IT'S TIME YOU STOPPED WORKING FOR THE COMMITTEE! WHAT POST HAVE THEY OFFERED YOU?

WELL, IT HASN'T BEEN ANNOUNCED YET, SO YOU CAN'T TELL ANYONE, BUT I'M GOING TO BE DEPUTY ASSISTANT TO THE ASSISTANT ATTORNEY GENERAL!

GRACIOUS, DEAR! YOU'LL BE ABSOLUTE-LY DRIPPING WITH POWER!
UM... I GUESS SO. BUT I'LL STILL BE DRIV-ING MY OLD BATTERED VOLVO.
©B Trudeau

HELLO?
JOANIE? HI, IT'S BARKLEY BERNAUER!

BARKLEY BERNAUER? YOU'RE KIDDING.
BLAST FROM THE PAST, EH? HEY, I READ ABOUT YOUR APPOINT-MENT IN THE POST! CONGRATS!

UM... THANKS, BARKLEY.
LISTEN, I WAS THINKING—WE SHOULD GET TO-GETHER SOMETIME. IT'S BEEN AGES!

17 YEARS, IN FACT.
THAT LONG? THEN WE GOTTA DO LUNCH!
©B Trudeau

RING! RING!
HI, THIS IS JOANIE. I'M NOT IN RIGHT NOW...

IF YOU'RE SOMEONE I HAVEN'T HEARD FROM IN YEARS, AND YOU'RE CALLING BECAUSE OF MY NEW JOB, THANKS AND GOODBYE.

IF, ON THE OTHER HAND, YOU'RE AN F.O.J., PLEASE LEAVE A MESSAGE AND I'LL CALL YOU RIGHT BACK! BYE! BEEP!
©B Trudeau

F.O.J.?
FRIEND OF JOANIE. THEY KNOW WHO THEY ARE.

SO WHATCHA WORKING ON THESE DAYS?
I'M REVISITING THE KIMBERLIN CASE. REMEMBER THE GUY WHO SAID HE SOLD POT TO QUAYLE?
TAP! TAP!

HE GOT THROWN IN THE HOLE AND HAD **YEARS** ADDED TO HIS SENTENCE, DESPITE BEING A MODEL PRISONER. THE GUY'S BEEN LIVING ONE LONG NIGHTMARE.

THE INSPECTOR GENERAL IS INVESTIGATING, BUT MEANWHILE, KIMBERLIN'S STILL IN JAIL. WHAT HE DESPERATELY NEEDS IS A CHAMPION IN THE NEW JUSTICE DEPARTMENT!

SAY...
THE LINE FORMS AT THE REAR.
©B. Trudeau

KIMBERLIN'S BECOME THE FORGOTTEN MAN, JOANIE. HE'S LONG SINCE DONE HIS TIME, BUT THE BUSHIES PUT THE FIX IN ON HIS PAROLE...

BOTH AMNESTY INTERNATIONAL AND HUMAN RIGHTS WATCH ARE CONSIDERING DESIGNATING HIM A POLITICAL PRISONER. YOU **GOTTA** TAKE UP KIMBERLIN'S CASE!

I DON'T KNOW, RICK. WITH ZOE GONE, I'M NOT EVEN SURE I STILL HAVE A JOB. AND IF I DO, I'VE GOT MY OWN CAUSES TO CHAMPION...
LIKE WHAT?

WELL, LIKE, I'M TRYING TO GET MIKE MILKEN BACK **INTO** JAIL.
MAYBE THEY COULD SWITCH PLACES.
©B. Trudeau

SO WHAT DO YOU SAY, BABE? CAN YOU BRING UP THE KIMBERLIN CASE?

I'LL THINK ABOUT IT, RICK. I HAVE TO START SLOWLY. I DON'T REALLY KNOW THE ROPES AT JUSTICE...

AND THAT'S ASSUMING I STILL HAVE A JOB. THE FALLOUT FROM THE NANNY CRISIS SEEMS TO BE NEVER-ENDING...

I WANT SOCIAL SECURITY.
RIGHT. WANT ME TO START TURNING DOWN YOUR BED, TOO?
©B. Trudeau

B.D., I'VE REACHED A DECISION. I WANT TO GO LEGIT!

I'M TIRED OF BEING IN THE UNDERGROUND ECONOMY, TIRED OF PULLING 18-HOUR SHIFTS, TIRED OF NOT BEING ABLE TO PILE UP MY OWN CREDIT CARD DEBT!

I'VE DECIDED TO GO STRAIGHT! TO GET A SOCIAL SECURITY NUMBER, TO BECOME A PROUD, STAND-UP, TAX-PAYING MEMBER OF THE **WORK FORCE!**

CONGRATULATIONS. YOU'RE FIRED.
HEY, C'MON, MAN, IT'S LONELY OFF-BOOK. I CAN'T SPEAK SPANISH.
GB Trudeau

BOOPSIE? I'M TIRED OF BEING THIS FAMILY'S DIRTY LITTLE SECRET! I WANT TO BE ON THE BOOKS!

FROM NOW ON, I **DEMAND** THAT YOU START PAYING MY CITY, STATE, FEDERAL AND SOCIAL SECURITY TAXES!

ZONKER, THAT'S JUST SILLY.
SILLY? WHY IS IT **SILLY,** IF I MAY ASK?
GB Trudeau

ZONKER, WE DON'T PAY YOU ANYTHING!
THAT'S **ANOTHER** THING!

I DON'T KNOW ABOUT YOUR PARENTS, SAM— THEY DON'T SEEM TO GET IT!

TWO LONG MONTHS OF LOYAL SERVICE TO THIS FAMILY, AND WHAT DO I HAVE TO SHOW FOR IT? NOTHING! NO SAVINGS, NO PENSION, NO HEALTH PLAN...

IT'S AS IF I DON'T EVEN EXIST! AND ALL BECAUSE YOUR MOM AND DAD WANT TO AVOID PAYING TAXES ON A SALARY!

WHY DON'T YOU STEAL THE SILVERWARE?
SAME KINDA DEAL. I'D HAVE TO PAY TAXES ON IT.
GB Trudeau

IT'S JUST AN OUTRAGE, SAM— I'VE BEEN A PROFESSIONAL NANNY FOR FOUR YEARS NOW, AND I'M **STILL** OFF-BOOK! I'VE NEVER BEEN PUT INTO THE SYSTEM!

WITHOUT A SOCIAL SECURITY NUMBER, YOU HAVE NO PAST AND YOU HAVE NO FUTURE! I'LL TELL YOU, THIS ALIEN BUSINESS HAS REALLY RAISED MY CONSCIOUSNESS!

ARE YOU AN ALIEN, ZONKER?
NO, NO, I'M AN EARTHLING! BUT I CAN'T **PROVE** IT!

LOOK, BOOPSIE, I KNOW YOU CAN'T SWING A REAL SALARY, SO JUST PAY TAX ON MY ROOM AND BOARD. WHAT I WANT IS A PENSION! THE TRUTH IS, I CAN'T STOP THINKING ABOUT TOMORROW!

BRRG!
I DUNNO, Z, I... HOLD ON...
HOW ABOUT IT? DEAL?

HELLO?
HELLO, MS. BOOPSTEIN? THIS IS "VARIETY." WE'RE DOING A BIG STORY ON MOVIE PEOPLE WHO AVOID PAYING TAXES FOR THEIR DOMESTIC HELP!

DEAL.
GOOD OL' UNCLE DUKE.

HEY... HARRIS! WHERE HAVE YOU **BEEN** ALL DAY? BOOPSIE AND I WANTED TO GO OUT!
SORRY, B.D.—I WAS OUT LOOKING AT THE GOLDEN CLOUDS RETIREMENT COMMUNITY!
SPORTS

SAY WHAT?
IT'S AN AWESOME SET-UP! GOLF, TENNIS, BEACH, POOL—THE WORKS! CHECK OUT THIS BROCHURE...

LITTLE EARLY TO BE SHOPPING FOR HOMES, ISN'T IT? YOUR PENSION DOESN'T KICK IN UNTIL YOU'RE 65.
65? WAIT A MINUTE! I CAN'T RETIRE UNTIL I'M **65?**

THAT'S RIGHT. WHEN'D YOU HAVE IN MIND?
NEXT SATURDAY. NO **WONDER** THERE WERE SO MANY OLD PEOPLE...
SPORTS

OUR TURN HAS COME, J.J.! TIME TO PUT UP OR SHUT UP! TIME TO TURN THIS COUNTRY AROUND, TO RECLAIM ITS GREATNESS! GOD GO WITH YOU, MR. C!

DON'T YOU FEEL LIKE IT'S A NEW DAWN, B.D.? LIKE THE PLANETS ARE IN PERFECT ALIGNMENT?
UH-HUH...

READY TO ROLL UP YOUR SLEEVES?
ARE YOU KIDDING? MY WHOLE **LIFE** HAS LED UP TO WORKING FOR THIS ADMINIS-TRATION!

GET READY FOR PRIDE, CAMPERS! GET READY FOR RESPONSIBILITY! GET READY FOR SOCIAL JUS-TICE! THE BIG GUY IS **ON THE MOVE!**

I'LL TELL YOU ONE THING: WE'RE AT A REAL CROSSROADS! THE WHOLE **IDEA** OF AMERICA IS ON THE LINE! IT'S NOW OR **NEVER!**

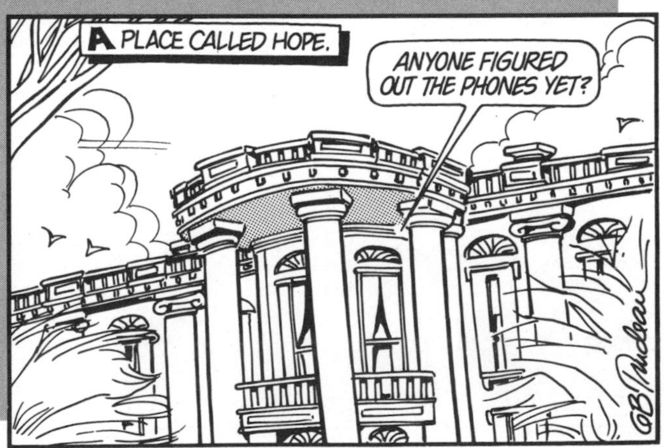
A PLACE CALLED HOPE.
ANYONE FIGURED OUT THE PHONES YET?
GBTrudeau

THIS SPACE FOR RENT

YOUR MESSAGE HERE

YOUR PERSONAL MESSAGE HERE

YOUR CLASSIFIED AD HERE

YOUR AD HERE

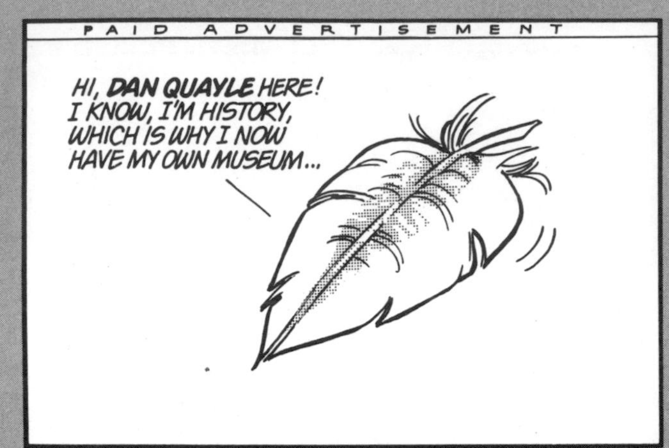
PAID ADVERTISEMENT
HI, DAN QUAYLE HERE! I KNOW, I'M HISTORY, WHICH IS WHY I NOW HAVE MY OWN MUSEUM...

YES, THE DAN QUAYLE CENTER AND LIBERRY, SCHEDULED TO OPEN IN MY HOMETOWN OF HUNTINGTON, INDIANA, LATER THIS SPRING!
DAN QUAYLE CENTER AND LIBERRY

FUN FOR THE WHOLE FAMILY, THE QUAYLE CENTER AND LIBERRY WILL HOUSE SUCH QUAYLE MEMORABILIA AS MY LITTLE LEAGUE UNIFORM, MY PERSONAL BIBLE, MY LAW DEGREE...
TO THE LIBERRY

...AND MORE THAN 6,000 FAMILY PHOTOS, DOCUMENTS, AND PERSONAL EFFECTS!

YES, THE QUAYLE CENTER WILL BE A REAL MUSEUM, JUST LIKE THE SMITH-SONIAN, ONLY WITH-OUT THE BORING PARTS! SO PACK UP THE KIDS AND COME ON DOWN! CALL NOW FOR RESER-VATIONS!
PAID ADVERTISEMENT

HE CAN ACTUALLY BOOK SPACE FROM US?
WE DON'T HAVE ANY CHOICE, Z. WE'RE CARRYING A LOT OF OVERHEAD.
©B Trudeau

WELL, WE'RE ON OUR WAY!
HOW'S THAT, Z?

WITH CLINTON! A BOLD NEW BEGINNING! CAUGHT THE EXCITEMENT YET?
CLINTON WHO?

CLINTON. BILL CLINTON.
NEVER HEARD OF HIM.

WHAT DO YOU MEAN, YOU'VE NEVER HEARD OF HIM?
JUST THAT. THE NAME MEANS NOTHING TO ME.

BUT... BUT HOW CAN THAT BE? YOU'RE USUALLY SO UP ON THINGS...
TRUE.

I KNOW! THIS MUST BE AN OLD EPISODE! IS THIS A RE-RUN?
LEMME CHECK... YUP! 1989!
GB Trudeau
© 1989 G.B. Trudeau/Univ. Press Synd.